Abs Revealed

JONATHAN ROSS

Library of Congress Cataloging-in-Publication Data

Ross, Jonathan, 1970-
  Abs revealed / Jonathan Ross.
    p. cm.
  ISBN-13: 978-0-7360-8650-9 (soft cover)
  ISBN-10: 0-7360-8650-1 (soft cover)
  1. Abdominal exercises. 2. Reducing exercises. 3. Physical fitness. I.
Title.
  GV508.R67 2010
  613.7'1886--dc22

                          2010021977

ISBN-10: 0-7360-8650-1 (print)
ISBN-13: 978-0-7360-8650-9 (print)

The Web addresses cited in this text were current as of August, 2010, unless otherwise noted.

Acquisitions Editor: Justin Klug; **Developmental Editor:** Heather Healy; **Assistant Editors:** Michael Bishop and Elizabeth Evans; **Copyeditor:** Joy Wotherspoon; **Permission Manager:** Martha Gullo; **Graphic Designer:** Bob Reuther; **Graphic Artist:** Tara Welsch; **Cover Designer:** Keith Blomberg; **Photographer (cover and interior):** Neil Bernstein; **Visual Production Assistant:** Joyce Brumfield; **Photo Production Manager:** Jason Allen; **Art Manager:** Kelly Hendren; **Associate Art Manager:** Alan L. Wilborn; **Illustrations:** © Human Kinetics unless otherwise indicated; **Printer:** United Graphics

We thank Catalyst Fitness in Woodstock, Georgia, for assistance in providing the location for the photo shoot for this book.

Human Kinetics books are available at special discounts for bulk purchase. Special editions or book excerpts can also be created to specification. For details, contact the Special Sales Manager at Human Kinetics.

Printed in the United States of America   10 9 8 7 6 5 4 3 2 1

The paper in this book is certified under a sustainable forestry program.

Human Kinetics
Web site: www.HumanKinetics.com

United States: Human Kinetics
P.O. Box 5076
Champaign, IL 61825-5076
800-747-4457
e-mail: humank@hkusa.com

Canada: Human Kinetics
475 Devonshire Road Unit 100
Windsor, ON N8Y 2L5
800-465-7301 (in Canada only)
e-mail: info@hkcanada.com

Europe: Human Kinetics
107 Bradford Road
Stanningley
Leeds LS28 6AT, United Kingdom
+44 (0) 113 255 5665
e-mail: hk@hkeurope.com

Australia: Human Kinetics
57A Price Avenue
Lower Mitcham, South Australia 5062
08 8372 0999
e-mail: info@hkaustralia.com

New Zealand: Human Kinetics
P.O. Box 80
Torrens Park, South Australia 5062
0800 222 062
e-mail: info@hknewzealand.com

E4927

Contents

Exercise Finder

Exercise name	Floor (no equipment)	Basic equipment	Stability ball	TRX	Slide	Page number
Supine draw-in	●					44
Supine brace	●					45
Prone plank	●					46
Side plank	●					47
Reverse crunch with hand targets	●					48
Dead bug	●					49
Harder-than-it-looks (HTIL) crunch	●					50
Negative crunch with control	●					51
Quadruped draw-in with arm and leg movement (bird dog)	●					52
Reverse crunch from floor	●					70
Bicycle crunch	●					93
Reverse crunch from bench		Bench				71
Frozen bicycle		Bench or abdominal board				72
Hanging knee raise		Pull-up bar				73
Hanging leg raise		Pull-up bar				74
Flying bicycle crunch with medicine ball		Medicine ball				94
Hanging knee raise with a twist		Pull-up bar				95
Bar chop		Light barbell or weighted bar				96
Standing oblique crunch with cable		Pulley machine				97
BOSU double crunch		BOSU balance trainer				109
Roll-up on stability ball			●			53
Side plank on stability ball			●			54
Reverse crunch with stability ball			●			55
Semi-vise crunch with stability ball			●			56
Vise crunch with stability ball			●			57
Vise crunch with leg roll with stability ball			●			58
Leg drop with ball balance			●			59
Plank with elbows on stability ball			●			60
Plank with shins on stability ball			●			61
Crunch on stability ball			●			75
Offset-arm crunch on stability ball			●			76

If you want great abs, you have to know how to train them, but knowledge is not enough. Great abs require much more than just doing exercises and having strong abdominal muscles. You may have the best abs possible, but if they are blanketed by a layer of body fat, no one will see them. Underneath the skin and body fat, we all look like an anatomy chart. Consider sumo wrestlers. They are strong and they have lots of muscle, but do you want to look like them? Probably not. Their massive amounts of muscle are hidden by even greater amounts of fat. This book shows you how to get strong abs and how to reveal them.

For decades, abdominal training has consisted of specialized techniques, equipment, and supplements that treat the abdominals as if they were separate from the rest of your body. Thankfully, this stone age of abdominal training is now over. With *Abs Revealed*, you are entering the chiseled age. The abdominals are part of the machine of your body. Although you want that body to be visually appealing, you still need the machine to work well. Every movement you make involves some part of your abs; they are the engine of movement in your beautiful machine.

With this book, you will discover how to train your abdominals for show while learning where the abs are and what they do as well as strategies that help you show them off. You'll learn creative, cutting-edge exercises that work your abs like never before, combined with the latest thinking on how nutrition and aerobic training have a powerful effect on the appearance of your midsection. You'll discover the right place to begin based on your current fitness level, and you will receive a workout plan that lets you have a life outside of your workouts and accurate information that cuts through myths that undermine even the most committed exercisers. Get ready for workouts that are intelligent, efficient, and driven by results. The approach in *Abs Revealed* will help you start, progress through the exercises, and finish with stellar abdominals.

In part I, you'll find the core concepts, or the basic information you need to reach your results. In chapter 1, you'll learn about the anatomy of your abs in simple terms. You don't need to be an exercise scientist to understand how to put this information to work for your abs. Chapters 2 and 3 give you the most current thinking on the roles of aerobic training and nutrition for reducing fat to reveal your abdominals. The cutting-edge techniques for maximizing your aerobic training in chapter 2 make the most of *caloric quantity* (total calories burned in a workout) and *caloric quality* (calories burned from fat in a workout) using interval training. This approach will change the way you track cardio intensity. Instead of doing more cardio, you'll do it better. In chapter 3, food becomes the ally (rather than the enemy) of great abs. The right foods at the right times will power you through effective workouts. This chapter explains how to choose carbohydrate wisely, why choosing the right types of fat can actually propel you toward better muscle definition, and how to deliciously fuel your body. You'll never want to miss another meal!

Part II presents exercises you've never seen before. It also explains how to get the most out of the exercises and equipment to target the abs and how to modify each exercise. The exercises are designed around you—your abs and your body—in three phases. You will work toward the washboard in chapter 4 with exercises that use basic equipment or your own body for resistance. You know that your ab muscles work hard in exercises to create movement, but you might be surprised that they can work even harder to prevent movement. In chapter 5, the exercises use body weight and equipment to move in a single direction, mirroring the three actions of your spine. The exercises are designed to work your abs even harder with the stability, or anti-movement ability, that you developed in chapter 4. Finally, the exercises in chapter 6 combine multiple directions of movement, using all of your abs together for maximum results. This chapter presents many options for challenging your abs.

To achieve abdominal success, you need a strategy for putting it all together. Part III provides these tools. Chapter 7 presents great tips for setting goals and prioritizing your nutrition changes for the greatest effect. You will find a simple strategy for successfully using any amount of time you have. The process of sculpting your abs is broken down into three phases: Rock, Paper, and Scissors. In the Rock phase, you will lay down new, strong muscle and will begin reducing body fat with exercises from chapter 4. Next, as your layer of body fat thins in the Paper phase, you will take on greater challenges with exercises from chapter 5. Finally, you get cut in the Scissors phase with exercises from chapter 6. Each phase also deepens your commitment to your nutrition goals and aerobic training. Once you've revealed great abs on your body, you'll learn foolproof strategies in chapter 11 so you can maintain your results.

Throughout the text, you'll find pearls of training wisdom, nutrition nuggets, and insights from my many years as a fitness trainer. Along the way, you'll also enjoy an occasional look at many of the myths and misconceptions that can lead you away from the path toward great abs. *Abs Revealed* delivers the clarity you need while you pursue your best abdominals. Take a giant leap forward by removing the obstacles in the path to great abs! *Abs Revealed* gives you the tools you need to chisel the abs you want from the rock of your body.

Acknowledgments

I must acknowledge whatever or whoever gave me the strength to turn a personal tragedy into a positive result. It's an odd world where many people use tragic events in their lives as excuses for engaging in behaviors that only make their lives worse. My father's death from obesity led directly to my entry into a fitness career that has been nothing but wonderful.

Thank you to all the wonderful and intelligent people I have learned from over the years. I spent the early years of my fitness career learning as much as possible and surrounding myself with the best people in the fitness industry. It's truly a shame that many of them aren't household names because they should be. The well-worn phrase "standing on the shoulders of giants" is most appropriate in this case. What I absorbed from them planted seeds that eventually grew into many of the ideas, concepts, and fresh perspectives on fitness you will enjoy in this book.

A special thank you to all the clients and people over the years who said to me, "you should write that down," or constantly told me I should start writing. I finally got the message.

Thanks to all of the staff at Human Kinetics for helping me express my ideas in the best way possible and to produce a finished work we can all be proud of.

Thanks to the models who gave their time, expertise, and their abs for the images in this book.

Thanks to anyone who has ever taken anything I've said and used it to make their lives better. That's all I really want—to share information to help everyone reach their own potential.

PART I

Core Concepts

Stability and Strength for Show

Clients have asked me countless times while grabbing a part of the body, "What can I do to get this in shape?" Frequently, the body part in question is the abdominal area. Right or wrong, fitness programs often focus on the abdominals. This makes a certain amount of sense. After all, people with great abs never have bodies that are flabby or untrained everywhere else. However, plenty of people have big chests and thick guns but also have big bellies. Although many great exercises exist to develop the abdominals, you may find it difficult to make yours look the way you want.

Great abs are not merely strong. Most sumo wrestlers and power lifters have very strong arms and legs, but they couldn't lift much without strong abdominals. However, you probably don't want to look like them. Because the midsection is the first place that body fat goes to be stored and the last place that it leaves when calories are burned, the abdominals are the standard by which we judge our fitness level and by which others judge our sex appeal.

Mistakes in the Middle

Historically, the abdominals have been trained at random with many ineffective strategies that used either a lot of exercises or a lot of repetitions without much rhyme or reason. For example, many people do hundreds of crunches to target the abs, but they don't do similar numbers of squats, pull-ups, bench presses, or any other exercises to train other parts of the body. This style of training is essentially very low-intensity cardio for the abs. When reps are that high, performing crunches is no longer resistance training. By definition, resistance training is a short, high-intensity activity. If you take a couple minutes to do a set of anything, you're working aerobically. Another reason to avoid sets of 100 crunches is that repeated flexing of the spine can contribute to spinal disc injuries, such as herniation.

For decades, the abdominals have been trained ineffectively and incorrectly because we feel they are particularly important. We simply do more exercises for the abs than we do for any other body part. But although we give them favored treatment in our workouts, the abdominals don't know or care just how special they are to us. They are just one group of muscles among many in the human body and are subject to the same scientific rules that govern all other muscles. They don't get special treatment in terms of biology. They perform their job and then rest. They get stronger when taken past their current ability level and they get weaker if they are ignored. They are subject to the same rules of breakdown, recovery, and growth as all other muscles.

A New Approach

Taking a more intelligent and modern approach to training that avoids the mistakes of past exercise programs and ineffective equipment will give you abdominal muscles that look great. Even when we were young, we had the key to understanding the secret of having good abdominals, but we didn't know it at the time. Remember the song "Dem Bones" that we sang as kids?

> *The toe bone's connected to the ankle bone,*
> *The ankle bone's connected to the shin bone,*
> *The shin bone's connected to the knee bone,*
> *The knee bone's connected to the thigh bone,*
> *The thigh bone's connected to the hip bone. . .*

The lyrics to this traditional African-American spiritual might be a little spotty on the anatomical details, but they show us the way to effective training. The song that helped us learn body parts as kids also illustrates the major shift in thinking that is necessary to reveal your best abdominals: Everything is connected to everything else. You can drag an entire chain by grabbing and pulling a single link. Pulling on one link in the chain produces results for all the other links. Unless you barely touch it at all, you can't move a single link in isolation. When it comes to moving your body, remember that everything you move is connected to something else.

Think of it this way: A movie star who wins an Academy Award doesn't just say thanks and walk off the stage after receiving it. The actor begins listing the roles he played, both large and small, on his way to becoming a star and all the people who contributed to his success, including parents, old drama teachers, personal assistants, talent agents, and others behind the scenes. In fact, this litany of supporting roles often goes on so long that the orchestra must play to signal an end to the star's speech. Struggling actors who become stars do so only with the support of a massive group of people who are the true driving force of their success.

The same idea applies to your abs. To put on the best possible abdominal performance, you have to train the abs you can see and the ones you can't, or the supporting cast. Your six-pack is the star, but it needs a lot of support to be successful. The muscles under the six-pack are never seen, but they support the success of your washboard. Physiologists call these two groups of muscles the *inner unit* and the *outer unit*. Suppose you have the best snow jacket in the world. Even the best jacket in the world can't do its job properly if you wear it without any other clothing. The supportive layers worn underneath the jacket help it function properly. Your hidden layers of abdominal muscle have the same relationship with the visible layers on the surface.

You'll meet all the muscles soon enough, but before you do, remember that hidden abdominal stability yields visible abdominal strength, or a sculpted six-pack. Consider a bullwhip, with its firm, rigid handle and flexible tail. When striking a whip, the stability of the handle allows the force of the forward motion to flow smoothly through the lash to the tail, producing a dramatic result. Imagine what would happen if you tried to strike while holding the tail of the whip. No matter how hard you thrashed your arm, the other end of the whip would go nowhere. In the case of our training, stable inner ab muscles yield a dramatic result for the outer ab muscles, the arms, and the legs.

Anatomy of the Abdominals

The stars of the show are the main abdominal muscles: the rectus abdominis, the obliques (internal and external), and the transversus abdominis. However, in order to train more effectively, you need to make the distinction between the inner and outer abdominal muscles. As you review, remember this key concept: Outer muscles that are well developed and beautiful require inner muscles that are stable and capable. There's no point in putting on the world's greatest jacket if you're not going to wear a shirt underneath.

Outer Abdominal Muscles

The outer abdominal muscles include the rectus abdominis, the external obliques, the internal obliques, and the erector spinae. This entire series of muscles essentially surrounds the lower half of your torso and is, ideally, the most visible for great abs. These large abdominal muscles provide strength for movement and stability for preventing movement.

Rectus Abdominis

This outermost layer of abdominal muscle (see figure 1.1) makes up the six-pack and really serves as the tip of the iceberg when it comes to abdominal training. Everyone sees the six-pack, but the full story of the abdominals lies below the surface. The six-pack is actually an eight-pack, but you typically can't see the bottom two parts unless you are completely naked! The rectus abdominis is a long, thin muscle whose fibers run vertically down the body, beginning between the fifth and seventh ribs and ending at the pubic bone. It has eight bumps sticking out of a grid of flat tendons that bisect and run down the length of the muscle. This muscle flexes the trunk and moves the rib cage and pelvis closer together.

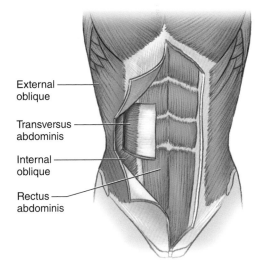

External oblique

Transversus abdominis

Internal oblique

Rectus abdominis

FIGURE 1.1 **The eight-pack of the rectus abdominis.**

Do Upper and Lower Abs Really Exist?

Much debate occurs over the existence of upper and lower abs. Anatomy purists correctly point out that the fibers of the rectus abdominis are one long length of muscle. On the other hand, nature doesn't like waste, so there must be a reason for the three sections of tendons that cut across the length of the muscle. For example, the biceps is also a single, long muscle, but it doesn't have tendons crosscutting its length.

Empirical evidence also exists to support differentiation within the muscle. You've likely done exercises that feel harder for the upper or the lower abs. During a workout, if you move your hips closer to your ribs, you're going to feel the lower portion of this muscle working harder than the upper portion is. If you move your ribs closer to your hips, the upper portion will dominate. Given this evidence, perhaps each part of the muscle differs in terms of its ability to contract. However, for the purpose of anatomy tests, the rectus abdominis is technically considered one muscle.

MYTHS AND MISCONCEPTIONS

MYTH: Crunches will give you flat abs.

REALITY: When training these muscles, you want to develop them just enough to make them look good when your body fat gets low.

If you make this muscle too strong and large, it will stick out and make your belly look bigger than it is. Ab training that consists only of sit-ups and crunches pushes this muscle out. You need a lot more than crunches for the best abs.

External Obliques

These muscles are visible, running diagonally from the ribs to the front of the pelvis (see figure 1.2) and the side of your eight-pack (rectus abdominis; refer to figure 1.1). Along with the internal obliques, they provide support and stability for the gut. Their action is to rotate your torso and to bend it sideways.

Internal Obliques

Although the depth of these muscles renders them invisible, they are no less important. They are one of the main stabilizers of your trunk. Like the external obliques, they lie on a diagonal, but they run in the opposite direction. They also rotate your torso. In torso rotation, motion is created by the internal obliques on the side you are turning toward and by the external obliques on the opposite side. As shown in figure 1.2, the fibers of the external oblique on one side lines up with the fibers of the internal oblique on the other side. For example, twisting to the left is a result of the actions of the internal obliques on the left and the external obliques on the right.

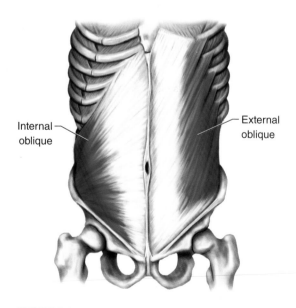

Internal oblique

External oblique

FIGURE 1.2 **The external and internal obliques.**

Use your hands to remember the alignment of these muscles. To trace the direction of the internal obliques, rest your hands on top of your lower ribs and then slide each hand down and around to your back pocket on the same side. To trace the direction of the external obliques, slide your hands down and in, moving from the lower ribs toward your belly button. For the internal obliques, your hands should move in toward your organs; for the external obliques, they should move out away from your organs.

Erector Spinae

The proper balance of strength and stability between the abdominal and back muscles makes for a truly well-built body. You can't have strong abs without a good back. The group of erector spinae muscles (see figure 1.3) is made up of the iliocostalis (top layer) and the longissimus (second layer). These back muscles run from the base of your skull, all the way down your spine, before finally connecting to the pelvis. You can feel these muscles in your lower back by locating the two vertical ridges that lie on either side of your spine. To find these ridges, stand up and bend slightly forward at the hips. If you feel only the bumps of the vertebrae in your spine, you are flexing too far forward. To straighten your spine, bend from your hips instead of your waist. These two layers of back muscles round out your cast of outer abdominal players.

Inner Abdominal Muscles

The behind-the-scenes muscles of the inner abdominals make the outer ones attractive and successful. Think of these muscles coordinating their actions to form a protective cylinder, or box for your organs, deep inside your trunk. They also provide a stable platform from which your outer ab muscles can push off when it is time for action.

Transversus Abdominis

Imagine your eight-pack abs as the Earth's surface. If you were to drill down to the core, you'd go through the rectus abdominis and the external and internal obliques, eventually arriving at the last solid layer— the transversus abdominis (TVA) muscle. This muscle forms the front of your inner-ab box and holds your gut flat. It runs from the sides of your eight-pack around your back, then attaches along your lower ribs and pelvis (see figure 1.4). As shown in the figure, the fibers run horizontally, so when they contract, you feel as if a belt is tightening around your middle. In fact, this muscle sort of looks like the championship belt of a boxer or professional wrestler, and your eight-pack is the shiny buckle!

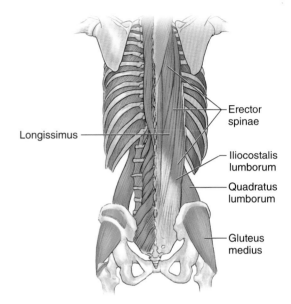

FIGURE 1.3 The muscles of the erector spinae.

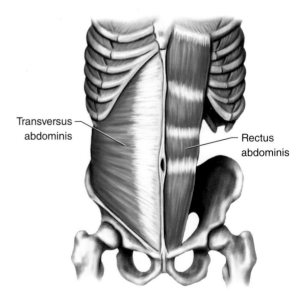

FIGURE 1.4 The fibers of the transversus abdominis run horizontally like a belt from the connective tissue that lies underneath the rectus abdominis muscle.

MYTHS AND MISCONCEPTIONS

MISCONCEPTION: Weight belts provide support for the back during lifting.

REALITY: The transversus abdominis works with the internal obliques to make a natural weight belt.

Wearing a weight belt causes your TVA to push out against the belt—exactly the opposite of what you want it to do during a lift. Weight belts should only be used when performing maximal lifts, such as those done by power lifters. In all other situations, training with a weight belt is a surefire way to make you weaker. Employees at home-improvement stores sometimes wear weight belts during their shifts to protect the company. If they hurt their backs at home because their inner abs are weak from using the belt, it won't cost the company as much money.

Quadratus Lumborum

The quadratus lumborum (QL) muscle runs from your bottom (12th) rib, along either side of your lumbar vertebrae, to the top of the pelvis (refer to figure 1.3). It stabilizes the spine and pelvis and plays a large part in any sideway-bending movement. Without a functioning QL, you probably wouldn't even be able to walk. Imagine the open space between the bottom rib and the top of the pelvis on skeletons you may have seen at Halloween or in science class. The QL muscle fills in this space.

Diaphragm

You probably know that the diaphragm is involved in breathing and speaking, but what does that really mean? When you take a full, deep breath, the diaphragm (see figure 1.5) essentially pushes down on your guts to make room for your lungs to expand. During exercise, the diaphragm pushes down, the TVA pushes in, and the QL compresses your organs tight against the spine to protect it. That's right—your inner ab muscles essentially shove your guts against your spine to keep the discs between your vertebrae from sliding all over the place.

If all these inner ab muscles, combined with the internal obliques and the TVA, are so important for rotating and stabilizing your spine, why are they almost never featured in traditional ab books and routines? The answer is simply because you can't see them. However, if the muscles that stabilize your spine are weak, your back will also be weak, preventing you from working your abs hard.

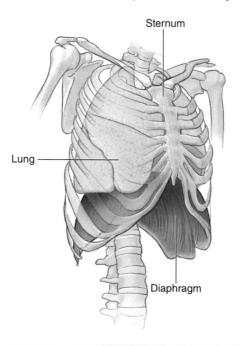

Sternum

Lung

Diaphragm

FIGURE 1.5   **The diaphragm muscle pushes down to clear space for the lungs.**

Pelvic Floor

Finally, the pelvic floor (see figure 1.6) literally keeps your guts from falling out. It pulls tight against the hip bones to keep the bottom of your protective organ box in place whenever you move or exert yourself.

You now know where your abs are and what they do, what the relationship between the inner and outer abs is, and why your abs must be trained with the rest of your muscles for the greatest success. Next, it's time to discuss cardio, one of the most confusing topics pertaining to great abs!

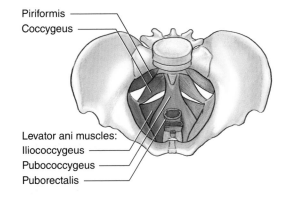

Piriformis

Coccygeus

Levator ani muscles:

Iliococcygeus

Pubococcygeus

Puborectalis

FIGURE 1.6   **The pelvic floor muscles function as the bottom of the barrel by holding your organs.**

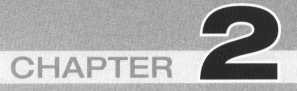

The Power of Cardio

Cardio is often misunderstood and is one of the most misused forms of exercise for just about any goal. To display the best abdominals, you must know how to use appropriate nutrition and exercise. Before you can unleash the power of cardio, you must address the widespread confusion and uncertainty about cardio training. Stop getting sidetracked or distracted by all the cardio clutter that is bouncing around your brain. After discrediting the myths, clearing up the confusion, and setting the record straight, you will know exactly what to do to make your abs pop out. Good information can be undone by bad, and it's time to take out the trash!

Confusion About Cardio

Cardio commonly refers to any activity that uses your cardiorespiratory system (heart, lungs, arteries, veins, and blood) to produce and deliver the energy for movement. In general, any activity you sustain beyond three minutes must be primarily aerobic in nature. *Aerobic training* is the term commonly used to describe activity that uses oxygen as the primary source of fuel. A broader definition of aerobic training is activity that improves the body's oxygen consumption, essentially making the cardiorespiratory system better at its job. Conversely, *anaerobic training* is the term commonly used to describe activity that does not use oxygen as the primary source of energy. In this case, the primary fuel source is carbohydrate.

Although the distinction between these two terms seems simple enough, nothing in them implies exclusivity. Aerobic training does not mean *only with oxygen*, just as anaerobic training does not mean *only with carbohydrate*. With a few extreme exceptions, you always use a mix of both. The terms simply define which source of energy provides the majority (51 percent or more) of fuel for activity. Too often, a given form of activity is presented as either aerobic or anaerobic. However, this either-or categorization of exercise may not accurately reflect what is happening in your body.

Most problems with our understanding of cardio, and exercise in general, stem from our curious tendency to oversimplify concepts with extreme terms. Given the wonder and complexity of the human body, just how simple can we really expect things to be? The two main misunderstandings are the fat-burning zone and intensity for effective workouts.

Fat-Burning Zone

When you step onto any common piece of cardio equipment, you're also stepping into a misleading concept—the existence of the fat-burning zone. The charts adorning the consoles of cardio equipment exist to provide some guidance on intensity during exercise. They typically show a graph with *age* labeled along the bottom and *percent of max heart rate* running up the vertical axis, and two colored bands. One is labeled the *fat-burning zone* and the other is called the *cardio zone*.

The design of these charts implies that you will only burn fat while working in the fat-burning zone. Likewise, you will only make your heart and lungs stronger while working in the cardio zone. As strange as it may seem, this ridiculous premise is based on truth. At lower intensities, you use more fat than carbohydrate for fuel. As intensity increases, your body continually adjusts the fuel mixture. Eventually, if intensity continues to rise, you will reach a point where your body uses more carbohydrate than fat for fuel. But what exactly does *more* mean?

If the premise that low-intensity activity burns more fat is carried out to its logical conclusion, the problems with this concept become glaring. According to this idea, you can burn a lot of fat by sitting on the couch all day. After all, sitting on the couch is the lowest form of activity. Your body uses calories even at rest, and in this case, most of the calories burned will come from fat. Of course, the problem is that you burn very few calories while at rest.

Here's another way to look at this problem. Suppose you received a gift of 80 percent of a friend's savings account. You'd be excited, right? If you then found out that your friend has only $100 in the bank, you might be disappointed. On the other hand, suppose you received a gift of 1 percent of a friend's savings account. You'd hardly be impressed. However, if you found out a million dollars are stored in the account, you'd be thrilled with your cut of $10,000! The same logic applies to your body. If most of your calories come from fat and you only burn a small number of them, you won't get anywhere in terms of fitness. To shore up your defenses against the folly of the fat-burning zone, remember that a big percentage of small number is still a small number.

A kernel of truth does exist in the myth of the fat-burning zone, and it involves how your body uses the energy it has. Energy use in your body occurs on a spectrum. When you are less active, your body burns more fuel from fat than from carbohydrate, but it burns less fuel overall. As you increase the intensity of your activity, your body adjusts the fuel mixture, first by upping the fat use, and then by lowering it. This process gives rise to the misconception that activity at lower intensities burns more fat. Later, you'll learn a better way to interpret this information.

Instead of doing more cardio, do better cardio. If your cardio workout is more challenging, your results will be better. The solution for stripping away unwanted body fat lies in interval training, which has gained popularity in recent years

MYTHS AND MISCONCEPTIONS

MYTH: To get lean, you have to do more cardio.

REALITY: To get lean, you have to do better cardio.

When most people want to lose body fat or get in shape, you often hear them proclaim they need to do more cardio, meaning that they will spend more time on it. Is this the best approach? Without discussing how cardio impacts your body in terms of physiology, let's consider the time factor. The number one reason given for not exercising is lack of time. Although this point is seriously debatable, if you're reading this, you're already past that concern. You have committed the time to your training to get into better shape and to get the best abs possible. Is the best approach to devote more time to exercise? In a world pressed for time, why is the first choice for better fitness to work out longer?

because it works. When you alternate bouts of higher and lower effort, you can continuously work harder within a given span of time. You can work out harder for shorter periods of time and get better results than you would with long workouts.

Every move you make draws energy from one of three sources: the phosphagen system (think of this as your rocket fuel), the fast glycolytic system (think of this as automobile fuel), and the oxidative system (similar to battery power). The first two systems are anaerobic in nature and the third is aerobic. Let's take a closer look at each of these systems to understand how they provide the fuel for various types of activity.

- **Rocket fuel (phosphagen system).** This system dominates when you perform a short-duration, high-intensity effort. It produces maximum power (90 to 100 percent of your ability), but burns out quickly, lasting only between 10 and 15 seconds. If you keep going when this fuel source runs out, your body will forcibly decrease intensity and access the next energy system, essentially slowing down the rocket.

- **Automobile fuel (fast glycolytic system).** This is the dominant energy system for efforts of higher intensity (75 to 90 percent of your ability). It kicks in after 15 seconds of activity (after the rocket fuel is exhausted) and lasts at least two minutes, but can go as long as four minutes in elite athletes.

- **Battery power (oxidative or aerobic system).** This is the main source of energy when you perform at 75 percent or less of your ability. It dominates anytime sustained activity lasts longer than the three-minute limit on automobile fuel.

This information should demystify the idea of the exclusive fat-burning zone. Now you know what's really going on. Your body uses carbohydrate and fat (with oxygen) through three energy systems to supply the fuel for activity. It simply adjusts the mixture, moment to moment, based on the physical demands of your activity. Your body is very smart.

What does all this mean for your workouts? If you're reading this book, your goal for cardio training is to use fat as a fuel source to define your abs (and other muscles, of course). You will discover exactly how to do this soon, but we still have another big problem with cardio that must be resolved.

Finding the Right Intensity

With the fat-burning zone out of the way, turn your attention to tracking intensity during cardio workouts. For decades, many formulas have been used to determine appropriate intensities for training. In fact, every year or two, a diligent team of physiologists does more research to further refine the methods, and a different version of these formulas becomes the new standard.

Let's examine some of the problems with these formulas. Take another look at the chart that appears on many cardio machines. The horizontal axis tracks age, and the vertical axis lists a percentage of maximum heart rate (MHR). The first problem should be obvious: Age alone does not determine fitness. A 30-year-old Ironman triathlete and a 30-year-old couch potato may both use cardio machines, but these two men cannot possibly have the same training range. The formula on the chart simply subtracts your age from the number 220 to determine MHR. It is so inaccurate that you'd be better off simply gauging how you feel during the workout. Some people fear that their chests will explode if they surpass their MHR. In this case, bad information is worse than no information.

Although other formulas take a step in the right direction, they are still troublesome. Some try to vary the contribution of age in the formula, while others use a measure of resting heart rate (RHR). These methods are more specific to the individual, especially with the use of RHR, reducing the error. However, all these formulas have one major issue. They start from the seriously questionable assumption that MHR is a fixed quantity. The following factors all affect and determine MHR:

- Genetics
- Heart size (different sizes of hearts do exist, and size does matter)
- Altitude where the training occurs
- Type of activity being performed

In addition to the influence of these factors, the use of MHR poorly correlates with performance, which varies even among people of the same age. As a result, your MHR is highly specific to you, factoring in the nature and location of your activity. The bottom line is that, as a measuring tool for exercise intensity, MHR is a mess. You need metabolism-based cardio training. Research has shown that some metabolic markers determine key crossover points in your body's use of fuel during exercise. Remember that the main goal of cardio workouts is to preferentially use fat as a fuel source to help bring out your abs.

Take a peek inside your body during exercise to discover how to best tap into fat stores. Imagine the following scenario. It's a beautiful day, and you head out for a walk. You start off on your leisurely stroll, enjoying the scenery. After a while, you realize that you have lost track of time and you need to get home to get ready for your workout. You quicken your pace and walk with purpose. In this situation, your body increases its use of fat and calories. You encounter a dog that looks a bit suspicious. You don't want to take any chances, so you start running to put some space between you and the dog. You're moving at a pace that you could sustain for a while. Now, your body increases its use of calories and fat a bit more. Suddenly, a thug with a knife appears and attempts to mug you. You take off, running at top speed. In this situation, your body seriously decreases its use of fat and begins burning a lot of carbohydrate to fuel the big effort. This scenario demonstrates how changes in intensity affect which energy system your body uses. It also suggests that you might consider moving to a different neighborhood.

Table 2.1 summarizes the energy contributions from fat and carbohydrate for various intensity levels. During rest, you aren't burning many calories, but most of those that are burned come from fat. When moving at low intensity, your need for calories goes up, but the demand isn't yet big enough to significantly call on carbohydrate, so fat use also goes up. At medium intensity, the contribution of calories shifts from fat to carbohydrate. Note that, due to the higher intensity, you are now burning more calories. As intensity continues to rise, you will decrease your fat use and increase your carbohydrate use.

With the goal of reducing your body-fat levels to display great abs, you want to use as many calories from fat per minute of exercise as possible. Essentially, you want to optimize both calorie and fat burning. To do this, you need to find the point at which your body crosses over from using fat to using carbohydrate. This is called ventilatory threshold one (VT1). This point of transition or metabolic crossover, shown in figure 2.1, is what you should be most interested in. You can measure it quite accurately during exercise with proper equipment for metabolic analysis, but you don't need breathing masks and a team of university scientists to pin down your metabolic crossover. All you need to figure it out is a simple test based on your breathing.

When exercising, the heart rate (HR) at which your breathing rate and depth of breathing first make speaking uncomfortable or challenging is your VT1. During the test, you will attempt to speak continuously for 30 seconds as the intensity of your activity becomes progressively more challenging. Since it is impossible

TABLE 2.1

Use of Fat and Carbohydrate for Varying Degrees of Intensity

Intensity level	Energy system	Percentage of calories burned from fat	Percentage of calories burned from carbohydrate
At rest	Battery power	50-60	40-50
Low intensity (walking or light jogging)	Battery power and automobile fuel	70-80	20-30
Medium intensity (jogging or running)	Automobile fuel	50	50
High intensity (running fast or sprinting)	Rocket fuel and automoblie fuel	1-20	80-99

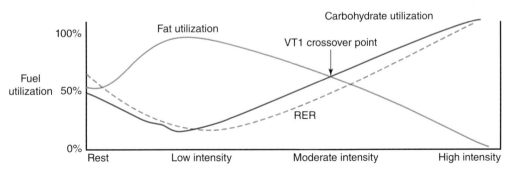

FIGURE 2.1   Fat and carbohydrate use at varying exercise intensities.

Adapted, by permission, from F. Comana, 2008, Metabolic training: The new cardio programming model. Presented at the American Council on Exercise Symposium, 2008.

to talk for 30 seconds while holding your breath, this length of time will help you accurately locate your VT1 HR. At higher levels of effort, you will need to pause to take bigger breaths in order to keep talking. At slightly lower intensities, you could fake it, continuing to talk even though you are running out of air. The following process helps you find your VT1 heart rate. Use a cardio machine that you're already comfortable with. Either wear a HR monitor or use a machine with handles that can sense heart rate. (If you plan on using the handles, don't do the test on a treadmill, since holding the handles makes your running style unnatural at higher intensities.) It's helpful, although not necessary, to bring someone to talk with. This keeps everyone else in the gym from thinking you're talking to yourself.

1. Warm up at an intensity that keeps your heart rate under 120 beats per minute (HR <120 bpm).
2. Continue at that pace for three to five minutes.
3. Speak continuously for 30 seconds.
4. Note your HR during the last 15 seconds of talking.
5. Increase your intensity (by increasing speed, resistance, or incline) to elicit an increase in HR of approximately 5 bpm. Maintain this level for about a minute, and then repeat steps 3 and 4.
6. Repeat step 5 until you have reached your VT1 (when you can no longer speak comfortably).

Adapted, by permission, from F. Comana, 2008, Metabolic training: The new cardio programming model. Presented at the American Council on Exercise Symposium, 2008.

To ensure validity, it is best to script the 30 seconds of talking so you don't have to think about what to say. Thinking about your speech could cause pauses that invalidate the test. You can use either of the two scripts provided in figure 2.2. Be sure to say each word in the list. When you can't get through 30 seconds of continuous talking without pausing to take a breath, you've hit your VT1 HR. At lower intensities, you should be able to breathe and talk without interrupting the flow of words.

The following example shows how you can conduct the test. Please note that your VT1 HR may be higher or lower than this example. Also, the speeds used on the treadmill and the heart rates listed are not meant to serve as a recommendations or reference values. This example is merely shows the sequence of events for the test.

1. Johnny Cutgut starts on the treadmill at 4.5 mph (7 kmph) and maintains a stable heart rate of 115 bpm.
2. He continues at this pace for 3 to 5 minutes.
3. Speed is increased to 5.5 mph (9 kmph). After about a minute, Johnny's HR is stable at 124 bpm. He begins reading through the civilian alphabet script and completes 30 seconds of talking.
4. Speed is increased to 6.0 mph (10 kmph). After about a minute, Johnny's HR is stable at 129 bpm. Again, he reads the script and completes 30 seconds of talking.
5. Speed is increased to 6.5 mph (10.5 kmph). After about a minute, Johnny's HR is stable at 135 bpm. He reads the script and completes the 30 seconds, but he pauses several times during the last 15 seconds. At this time, his heart rate was 140 bpm. This is his VT1 HR.

FIGURE 2.2

Scripts for VT1 HR Test

Copy these scripts for your VT1 HR test. Use the list you are more comfortable with.
Move through the alphabet, reading the words on each line.

Civilian alphabet script	Military alphabet script
A is for Apple	A is for Alpha
B is for Boy	B is for Bravo
C is for Cat	C is for Charlie
D is for Dog	D is for Delta
E is for Egg	E is for Echo
F is for Fish	F is for Foxtrot
G is for Girl	G is for Golf
H is for Hand	H is for Hotel
I is for Ice cream	I is for India
J is for Jet	J is for Juliet
K is for Kite	K is for Kilo
L is for Lamp	L is for Lima
M is for Man	M is for Mike
N is for Nose	N is for November
O is for Orange	O is for Oscar
P is for Pen	P is for Papa
Q is for Queen	Q is for Quebec
R is for Rain	R is for Romeo
S is for Sugar	S is for Sierra
T is for Tree	T is for Tango
U is for Umbrella	U is for Uniform
V is for Van	V is for Victor
W is for Water	W is for Whiskey
X is for Xmas	X is for Xray
Y is for Yellow	Y is for Yankee
Z is for Zoo	Z is for Zulu
Repeat list if time remains.	*Repeat list if time remains.*

From J. Ross, 2011, *Abs Revealed* (Champaign, IL: Human Kinetics).

To use your VT1 HR in training, you will move your intensity between two levels, or zones, that are located just above and below your crossover point. Zone 1 ranges from 10 bpm below your VT1 HR to your VT1 HR. Zone 2 starts at your VT1 HR and goes up to 10 bpm above it. In our sample test, the VT1 HR was measured to be 140 bpm. So, Johnny's zone 1 would be 130 to 140 bpm and his zone 2 would be 140 to 150 bpm. You will move your intensity between these two zones for different amounts of time during your workouts to optimize your use of both fat and total calories. Chapters 8 through 10, which discuss programming, provide specific instructions for this method of training.

Using your VT1 HR to track intensity is a smart approach to fat loss when you do cardio-interval training. However, you have another option for your cardio workouts called high-intensity interval training (HIIT). It eliminates the need to track intensity with heart rate by using full intensity. This type of interval training is broken up into short intervals of high-intensity effort followed by intervals of low-intensity effort, or even complete rest. This cycle simply repeats itself for a specified number of minutes.

Even though you will be well above your VT1 HR intensity during the high-effort intervals in this style of training, it is an effective method for fat loss, but for a different reason. HIIT creates what is sometimes called an *afterburn*. More specifically, after your HIIT workout is over, your metabolism stays slightly elevated for a significant amount of time. Your body basically freaks out and responds to the stress by bringing out hormones. In a nutshell, your body gets the message that you are in danger because you are moving fast. It's easy to see how our bodily response correlates with our human history as hunters. For rapid movement, we can't carry too much extra baggage.

Some research on these methods shows that this metabolic boost can last as long as an entire day. Consider what happens after you stop exercising in terms of your body's fuel use. While at rest, you get more energy from fat than from carbohydrate. If your metabolism is slightly elevated for a day or more after a workout, then you'll gradually consume a bit more fat hour by hour, which can have a powerful effect over time on your body-fat levels. The advantage of this method is that you can do it either outside or at the gym. You also eliminate the need to track your heart rate during the workout. The disadvantage is that it is extremely difficult, especially on certain pieces of cardio equipment. It also requires a high degree of psychological commitment. Chapters 8 through 10, which discuss programming, also provide specific instructions for this method of training.

To summarize, your cardio options for workouts in this book are as follows:

1. Zone training (ZT) with VT1 HR intervals
2. High-intensity interval training (HIIT)

You are free to use one method or the other exclusively, to mix and match, or to use them both. They both work for fat loss for different reasons. Choose based on your preference of training style or your access to equipment.

Timing Your Cardio Workouts

Should you do your cardio workouts before, after, or completely separately from weight training? Should you do them first thing in the morning on an empty stomach or during your lunch break? Does it really matter? This topic, like most others surrounding exercise (and human biology in general), lacks an easy answer. Human physiology is too complex and varied to define rules in narrow terms. You can decide what to do by filtering the rules through your own goals and what works for your body. To help you get it right, this section clarifies a number of cardio topics that are commonly confused, including using concurrent training and performing cardio first thing in the morning.

Concurrent Training

Concurrent training refers to performing your cardio and resistance training in the same exercise session. Performing cardio before weight training has little negative effect on upper-body exercises but can decrease performance of lower-body exercises. Performing cardio after weight training may help you access slightly higher amounts of fat for fuel. Recall that your body uses carbohydrate alone for fuel during resistance training. Most of this carbohydrate is stored in your muscles, but a little is also stored in your liver. If you perform your resistance training first, you tap into many of your body's carbohydrate stores. When you follow with cardio, an activity that uses fats and carbohydrate (depending on intensity), your body has less carbohydrate available, so it goes after more body fat. It always takes the easiest path to get the energy it needs. The research on this is not definitive, but I have seen this approach successfully change the body composition of numerous people.

For most people, separating cardio from resistance training is simply not an option. If you want to have any kind of personal life, you aren't crazy about the idea of generating twice the amount of dirty, sweaty laundry, or you don't have the luxury of time, you probably can't perform two separate workouts each day. Separate workouts may provide a physiological benefit, since you'll have more energy for each. Also, it's impossible to maximize all areas of fitness at the same time; you can't be great at both power lifting and triathlons. Doing your resistance training apart from cardio may give you a slightly better workout. However, the relatively small gain does not make up for the inconvenience that two daily workouts present for most people in the real world. Unless you are a bodybuilder or an athlete who is essentially paid to spend your days working on your body, separating the workouts will be a major hassle. Ultimately, though, the decision is up to you.

If you determine that concurrent training is the best option for you, you should perform cardiorespiratory training immediately after resistance training. Do not perform cardio immediately prior to resistance training, since this practice will negatively affect your second session. If you determine that concurrent training is not the best option for you, perform the cardio as a separate session. Whatever you decide, perform your test to determine your crossover point (VT1 HR) under the same conditions that you will use for performance. In other words, if you plan to do resistance training and cardio in the same session, you should do the test immediately after your resistance training. If you plan to separate your workouts, you should do the test apart from resistance training.

Cardio in the Morning

Many people wonder if they should do cardio workouts first thing in the morning. However, no single answer applies to everyone all the time. Determine the best choice for you by examining your goals and your body. Keep things practical. If a new study were published tomorrow that concluded that it is definitively best to do cardio first thing in the morning on an empty stomach, would it be the best approach for everyone? No, because some people would be totally miserable following this approach! You must know your body. If rising early and exercising on an empty stomach makes you feel like you are being torn from the womb, it is not a smart approach for you. You'll most likely either miss workouts or feel really irritable when you do them.

If you are considering this approach and are a naturally early riser, examine the question of whether it is a good idea to perform fasted cardio first thing in the morning. In general, fasting is not advisable because it compromises performance. If you consistently do resistance training and cardio and properly fuel your body with food, you will have a healthy and well-functioning metabolism. This means that you'll feel hungry within a short time of waking up. Your body will be looking for breakfast.

To help reveal your abs, your body should chew through stored fat. In order to do that, it needs a highly functioning metabolism. Your metabolism is like a campfire. If you fuel it at regular intervals, the fire generates a lot of heat and energy. If you starve it of fuel, it will still burn, but the dim, glowing embers will generate far less heat and energy than a well-fueled fire would. Furthermore, the contribution of exercise to the results you seek is determined primarily by your intensity. The factor of the specific time of day just isn't significant enough. Some people feel great and get great results from doing fasted morning cardio, but these people are the minority.

The key to great abs is a low storage of body fat. This means you should mobilize fat before, during, and after your workouts. *Mobilize* here simply means releasing fat from its place of storage in the fat cells into the blood stream, where it can be delivered to muscles for energy.

Once again, recall that the intensity of activity determines which source fuel is drawn from. Lower forms of activity use a higher percentage of fat as fuel. Sleeping is about the lowest form of activity you can do. Therefore, when you wake up, your amount of mobilized fat will be slightly elevated. Cardio of low to moderate intensity uses the circulating fat in the bloodstream and keeps it from being returned to storage in the fat cells. However, you need to take care to prevent hitting higher intensities, which shift your fuel mix to the carbohydrate side. Instead, morning workouts must be longer and of a consistent intensity. Low-intensity, steady-state cardio is just so boring! Your mind easily wanders, so you'd better have some great music, great reading, or an interesting TV show to watch.

Your main concern is body composition. In light of that, if you're doing everything else properly in terms of training and nutrition and are looking to make a bit of extra progress, you may benefit from performing cardio first thing in the morning on an empty stomach at low to moderate intensities. If you can do it and feel great, and you find that your results are better, it may be for you. However, the *if* in the previous sentence is a big one. Over the years, I have worked with numerous clients who have achieved great results, but only a few of them did fasted cardio in the morning. Those who did enjoyed it and found that it was a good fit for them, but I didn't instruct any of them to take this approach. Don't grudgingly force yourself to do something at a time of day that doesn't work for you just because you've heard it's supposed to be slightly better. The last factor you need to consider is your body type. If you are naturally lean and have a difficult time gaining muscle mass, fasted cardio in the morning is absolutely not for you, even if you do enjoy it.

The Recent Invention of Cardio

By now, you've seen how the widespread misuse and misunderstanding of cardio can prevent results. Sometimes, even when you know the truth, the constant barrage of outdated or incorrect ideas about cardio can weaken your defenses. The destructive voices can sneak into your head and tell you to do more cardio, to keep intensity low lest you leave the fat-burning zone, or to do cardio at a time that doesn't fit your goals or preferences.

A final, easy way to keep the nonsense from clouding your cardio plan and destroying your results is to consider this story. (You'll need it once your abs look great because people will be bugging you for advice. This way, you won't have to spout science at them.) Go back to a time before the existence of cardio machines, remote controls, office cubicles, riding lawn mowers, and even electricity. Humans were hunter-gatherers. They hunted and chased down prey, often moving at top speed to make the kill. They also evaded predators, whether man or beast, to avoid becoming prey themselves. When gathering, they often traveled long distances, foraging for berries, seeds, vegetables, and materials to build shelter. They hunted, gathered, and then rested after a hard day of work.

They didn't jog to stay in shape, run marathons, or do fun runs. There was very little need for long-distance, moderate-speed movement. Their movements either featured short efforts of very high intensity (hunting) or long, low-intensity efforts (gathering). Either way, every pound of fat they carried slowed them down, making it harder for them to move quickly for a short distance or slowly over a long distance. Conversely, every bit of muscle they added contributed mightily to their success as hunters, as gatherers, and ultimately, as a species. We carry this history of activity in our genes. It determines what our bodies are built to do. For millions of years, our blueprint for movement has been to go hard, fight for survival, and then rest.

In the last century or so, much of the need for survival-based movement has been engineered out of our daily lives. We can go an entire day without killing dinner or gathering sticks for fire or shelter without suffering the consequences of inactivity, but our bodies thrive on movement. Therefore, we have gyms and exercise equipment to help us supply our bodies with much-needed physical activity. After decades of neglect and inactivity, our bodies take on unwanted pounds of body fat. Eventually, we may become disgusted enough to shed the extra baggage. We begin to move again, but it's hard and uncomfortable. We've lost our physical edge. It's too difficult to work out hard enough to get results, so many people simply go through the motions. Health deteriorates and the body fat piles on.

For decades, society has told us that we need to do our cardio to lose weight. We've been inundated with the notion that low-intensity cardio is the way to go, so when we want to get in better shape, we simply do more cardio at the same ineffective intensity. When most people talk about their workouts, they focus on how much time they did, not on how much effort they put forth. After years of these recommendations, we're now more out of shape than we've ever been.

If you go to any history museum, you'll see statues of prehistoric humans with rippling abs, ropelike muscles, and low body fat. If you move your body like they did, you will literally look and feel like a lean, mean, fighting machine. Fortunately, our ancestors never encountered doughnuts or fried chicken. If they had, we might not be here today. What we eat is what we are made of. Hunter-gatherers had limited options. We aren't so lucky.

Development Through Diet

Eat your way to great abs. This might sound like the latest marketing pitch for a bogus diet plan, but nutrition is your main vehicle to great abs. Of course, working out is essential, but your food intake determines your body's response to your workouts. Think about it. You work out once each day, but you eat multiple times per day. Every time you do, you are moving either closer to your goals or farther away from them. Your ability to build muscle and to lose fat is a direct result of what is happening in your body and is an indication of what your body is made of. The things you eat make up every cell in your body. To meet your goals of developing and revealing great abdominals, you must fuel for great workouts and eat to enhance fat loss. You need to eat more of the foods that help promote fat loss and to avoid the ones that inhibit fat loss. Fortunately, you can still enjoy what you eat, but you may need to clarify what *enjoyment* means.

Great abs come from reducing the layer of fat on top of the ab muscles. Fat loss is a three-step process. You need to mobilize stored fat from fat cells, transport it through the blood stream to your muscles, and use it as fuel. Anything that disrupts one of the three steps will compromise your results. As you read through this chapter, keep two factors in mind:

1. Consider how any of the three steps of fat loss would be affected (either positively or negatively) by what you read.
2. Note which topics speak to you and your situation or habits the most.

Before you delve into the details, you need to start with a simple truth. You need fat, carbohydrate, and protein to live. No exceptions. You can safely ignore anyone who tells you to cut out one of those three things. Instead, you need to learn the difference between good carbohydrate and fat and bad carbohydrate and fat.

Fat

In the public consciousness and in popular diets, fat has been the whipping boy for decades, yet even with the advent of low-fat foods, people are gaining more body fat than ever. If the popular understanding of fat is correct, this shouldn't be happening. Clearly, something very basic with our attitudes about fat misses the mark, namely, the irrational perception that all fat is bad. The three main types of naturally occurring fat are saturated, monounsaturated, and polyunsaturated. You need all three types in order to be healthy, but you will need more details to determine where the types of fat you eat should come from.

A good place to start is by examining the names of the main types of fat. First, note that each type of fat contains the word *saturated*. The terms for the different types of fat describe the number of open spots where hydrogen molecules can bond along their carbon chains. Saturated fat has zero open spots and is therefore fully saturated with hydrogen. *Monounsaturated* fat has one spot open for hydrogen, while *polyunsaturated* fat has two or more spots open for hydrogen.

Although saturated fat is often vilified, it does serve a beneficial role in the body. It helps make hormones, which control just about everything in your body. However, you don't need this type of fat other than the amount needed for hormone production, so if the excess is not used for fuel, you will likely store it in your body. Unsaturated fat has a more diverse and useful role in your body. It coats your cells, cushions your joints, works to fight inflammation, and keeps your brain functioning properly. Therefore, a higher proportion of your fat intake should come from unsaturated fat. A simple way to achieve this proportion is to avoid adding any saturated fat to your food. For example, steer clear of full-fat dairy products, spread only the smallest amount of butter on your food, and don't cook anything with lard.

Most people don't realize this, but every fat or oil contains a mixture of saturated, monounsaturated, and polyunsaturated fat. We simply classify each fat or oil according to which of the three general types is most abundant. For example, olive oil is classified as a monounsaturated fat since this is the type that is most prevalent in its makeup, but it also contains polyunsaturated and saturated fat. You'll get adequate amounts of saturated fat by choosing seeds, nuts, and fatty fish.

Essential Fat

In the mad rush to eliminate fat from our daily intake, we've thrown the baby of unsaturated fat out with the bath water of saturated fat. Fat is neither friend nor foe, but its type makes all the difference in the world. Sorting through all the confusing terminology about healthy fat can be difficult. You'll encounter omega-3, omega-6, EPA, DHA, and EFA. Are you confused yet? Don't worry. The following overview will bring some clarity to the confusing terms. Essential fatty acids (EFAs) are fats that are necessary for life, but because our bodies can't make them, we have to eat them. Omega-3 and omega-6 are essential forms of polyunsaturated fat. They are the raw materials for the membranes that surround and protect every cell in your body, including those in your brain, eyes, and testes.

Fat is made up of chains of carbon. The numbers for omega fat simply refer to the number of carbons on the first open space (what chemists call a double bond) along the hydrogen bonds. Omega-3 fat has its first double bond at the third spot along the carbon chain, and omega-6 fat has its first double bond at the sixth spot. Omega-3 fat comes in three forms: alpha-linolenic acid (ALA), eicosapentaenoic acid (EPA), and docosahexaenoic acid (DHA). Omega-3 fat from plant sources typically takes the form of ALA, but omega-3 fat in fish typically takes the form of DHA. What does this mean to you? In your body, ALA is used to make EPA, which is then used to make DHA. But—and there's always a *but* with nutrition— the body's ability to convert ALA to DHA (through EPA) is limited, especially for men. DHA is essential for healthy organs, skin, joints, and brains. It also regulates the gene expression for hundreds of types of protein that make us who we are. You can see why it is essential! Include both ALA (plant sources) and DHA (marine sources) of omega-3 fat in your diet.

Omega-6 fat, also known as linoleic acid, is found in vegetable oils. It is used to make gamma-linolenic acid (GLA), which creates a host of other substances that are responsible for many of your body's functions. Some promote a healthy immune system, some limit inflammation, and some promote inflammation. If your body is getting enough omega-6 fat, it is smart enough to figure out exactly what to do with the resulting GLA.

Modern food processing uses a lot of omega-6 fat, so we typically consume 20 or 30 times more omega-6 than omega-3 fat. The ratio should be closer to 2:1 than 20:1 or 30:1, which is why so many nutritionists recommend that we eat more omega-3 fat. Table 3.1 shows the makeup of many common oils and types of fat.

TABLE 3.1

Makeup of Common Oils and Fat

Type of oil or fat	GRAMS OF FAT PER TABLESPOON				
	Saturated	Monounsaturated	Polyunsaturated		Other
			Omega-6	Omega-3	
Safflower oil*	0.8	10.2	2.0	0.0	0.6
Canola oil	1.0	8.9	2.7	1.3	0.7
Flaxseed oil	1.3	2.5	1.7	7.3	0.0
Sunflower oil*	1.4	2.7	8.9	0.0	0.6
Corn oil	1.7	3.3	7.3	0.1	0.6
Olive oil	1.9	10.0	1.3	0.1	0.5
Sesame oil	1.9	5.4	5.6	0.0	0.7
Soybean oil	2.0	3.2	6.9	0.9	0.6
Peanut oil	2.3	6.2	4.3	0.0	0.7
Cottonseed oil	3.5	2.4	7.0	0.0	0.7
Chicken fat	3.8	5.7	2.5	0.1	0.7
Lard (pork fat)	5.0	5.8	1.3	0.1	0.6
Beef tallow	6.4	5.4	0.4	0.1	0.5
Palm oil	6.7	5.0	1.2	0.0	0.7
Butter	7.2	3.3	0.3	0.2	0.5
Cocoa butter	8.1	4.5	0.4	0.0	0.6
Palm kernel oil	11.1	1.6	0.2	0.0	0.7
Coconut oil	11.8	0.8	0.2	0.0	0.8

*Safflower and sunflower oils can be high in either polyunsaturated or monounsaturated fat. Most bottled safflower oil and safflower oil used for commercial purposes is the high-monounsaturated variety shown here, but health-food stores sometimes sell the high-polyunsaturated variety. Bottled sunflower oil is usually high in polyunsaturated fat (as shown here), but most chips and other packaged foods use sunflower oil that is high in monounsaturated fat.

Adapted, by permission, from Center for Science in the Public Interest, 2002, "Face the fats," *Nutrition Action Newsletter* July/August 2002: 7. Sources: USDA Nutrient Database for Standard Reference (Release 22), the National Sunflower Association, and the Flax Council of Canada.

Trans Fat Should Be a Felony

You've probably heard of trans fat. Although you need a certain amount of other fat, you should avoid this fat like the plague. Trans fat is created by chemically altering an unsaturated fat so that it will last longer. The double bonds along the carbon chains of unsaturated fat make it more reactive to air and other ingredients. This reactive property is what makes this fat so good for your body! As a result, products with unsaturated fat spoil faster and have a shorter shelf life, which isn't good for cupcakes or doughnuts that might not be eaten for at least a month after they were made.

During processing, hydrogen molecules are forcibly added to the open spots of the unsaturated fat to transform it into a saturated fat. The resulting properties of trans fat make it very beneficial for food manufacturers and extremely toxic for humans. Trans fat wreaks havoc in your body by degrading healthy fat, taking up space in cells that healthy fat would normally occupy, and destroying the protective membranes around cells.

Research showing the dangers of trans fat began surfacing in the late 1970s. Many countries in Europe and Australia have already banned its production. However, the best the government in the United States has done so far is to require mandatory labeling of products that contain trans fat. Many local and state governments in the States are passing legislation to ban it, but this process takes a lot of effort in each jurisdiction. If you wait for the fat-cat politicians to pass smart nutrition laws, you'll wind up looking like them! Until laws change, you'll have to ban trans fat from your diet by reading food labels.

Don't trust banners proudly splashed on food labels that read "0 grams trans fat!" Read the ingredient list carefully. If you see the word *hydrogenated* before any type of oil, the product is not fit for human consumption. Be aware that current laws for food labeling favor commerce. According to current law, an amount of fat can be labeled as *zero* if it has fewer than 0.5 grams. This permits food makers to simply reduce serving sizes until the amount of trans fat per serving is under 0.5 grams, allowing them to proudly proclaim, "0 grams trans fat!"

Carbohydrate

Carbohydrate has taken a beating that is almost as severe as the criticism of fat. Once again, a simplistic yes-or-no approach does not work. The right kinds of carbohydrate, at the right times, will make you excited about your workouts and will provide the energy for your best effort. In contrast, the wrong kinds of carbohydrate, especially at certain times, will shut down fat burning and will enhance fat storage in your body. Just as with fat, your main nutrition goal is to consume healthier carbohydrate and to avoid the unhealthy types. Simply put, follow two main rules about carbohydrate to keep your body fat low and to reveal your abs:

1. Avoid sugar and processed carbohydrate (except after a workout) and seek out whole grains and fiber-rich carbohydrate, such as vegetables and fruit.
2. Eat whole-grain sources of carbohydrate earlier in the day.

Grain sources are the form of carbohydrate that helps you get up and go. They are typically much more calorie dense than vegetables and fruit. A food with a high caloric density has a large number of calories for the amount of space it takes up. Calorie density is a simple and important concept to remember when considering food choices. A 100-calorie serving of rice is rather small; you could easily plow through it and keep on going. However, a 100-calorie serving of broccoli is a massive stalk that you'd never eat in one sitting. This example shows how easily you can overeat grains. Foods with a high caloric density can help you power through workouts and recover from them. For optimal use, follow this rule: Eat carbohydrate from grains only at breakfast and after workouts. During the rest of the day, consume carbohydrate from fruits and vegetables.

Sugar and processed carbohydrate both inhibit hormones and enzymes that burn fat and promote fat storage. Either function alone would be bad enough, but the two together are a double whammy. These forms of carbohydrate are everywhere, from obvious junk foods like soda, doughnuts, candy, and sugar-coated cereal, to healthier foods like flavored yogurt, fruit juice, granola, and dried fruit. In general, grains pack a lot of energy into a small amount of food. Although they are good choice at breakfast to get you going, they are a poor choice at night when your body is winding down, making it ill-equipped hormonally to use this high-powered source of energy. Unless you work out at night, consuming even whole grains in the evening is a surefire way to promote fat storage.

Whole and Processed Grains

Finding sugar in foods is relatively easy—just look for the suffix -ose at the end of words in the ingredient list. But what are processed grains and how do they differ from whole grains? Let's start with wheat. A single kernel of wheat is composed of the germ (3 percent), the bran (14 percent), and the endosperm (83 percent). Each of these three parts must be present in a food for it to be labeled *whole grain*. They contribute a significant amount of vitamins and protein to the grain.

Processed (or *unwholy*) grains contain just the endosperm, the location of most of the calorie-rich carbohydrate. The milling process of grain into white flour removes the bran and the germ, as well as 21 vitamins and minerals! For example, white bread and other white-flour products, such as pretzels and crackers, that are made from the endosperm contain starches (a form of carbohydrate) and incomplete protein but few vitamins and minerals.

"Not to worry," say the food manufacturers, "we'll enrich our white bread with the missing vitamins and minerals." However, typically, only five vitamins and minerals (folic acid, iron, niacin, riboflavin, and thiamine) are added back, which hardly qualifies the product as enriched. Furthermore, the amounts of restored vitamins are less than the original composition of the grain. So, processed grains are either missing or deficient in some vital vitamins. Don't be fooled by names like *7 grain* or *12 grain* for bread or crackers. It doesn't matter how many different grains a product uses, if the grains aren't whole, it's junk food.

High-Fructose Corn Syrup

This caloric sweetener made from corn lurks in many foods, including soda, bread, and fruit juices. Many nutrition experts have concluded that high-fructose corn syrup (HFCS) is no worse than sugar. Since many people once felt that HFCS was more dangerous than sugar, this is supposed to be good news. However, sugar is terrible for you. The breaking news about HFCS means it is just as awful for you as sugar is. It might appear to be better to fall off a building from the 30th floor instead of from the 40th floor, but the result is still the same. HFCS is so pervasive and controversial because it is cheap! Since its production costs less than sugar's, more of it can be added to more products. The price of products that use HFCS stays low. Do you see a pattern here? Cheap sweeteners, cheap production, and cheap commercial costs add up to a cheap body if you eat them. Avoid HFCS and added sugar in the foods that you eat. If you just have to have sugar occasionally, eat it after a workout so that it helps aid in recovery.

Artificial Sweeteners

The topic of artificial sweeteners is hotly debated. Some people think that natural sweeteners are always better. Still, powdered sugar in any form is heavily refined and is, without question, not good for you. On the other hand, many artificial sweeteners were discovered while chemists who were creating new pesticides accidentally found that a certain compound tasted sweet. Some artificial sweeteners present legitimate concerns while others may be fine. We simply don't know what the effects of long-term use will be. Many people simply object to using artificial sweeteners on principle.

It's increasingly difficult to get straight information about the topic because much of what is out there comes either from organizations that stand to make or lose a lot of money from the verdict or from people with an agenda that erodes their objectivity. The Center for Science in the Public Interest (CSPI), a nonprofit group that seeks truth, is one of the most trustworthy organizations on these matters. At the time of this book's publication, the only sweetener the CSPI approves of is sucralose (commonly known as Splenda). However, concerns regarding the use of this product remain. After gathering the facts for yourself, your decision about which sweetener to use will be personal. Ultimately, the human body is smarter than you think. Regardless of whether it's real or artificial, sweetener is bad.

The best approach is to eliminate all artificial sweeteners from your diet and to consume as little sugar as possible. Why? Apparently, the perception of sweetness in the brain triggers a response in the body. Sweetness is one of the five primary flavors our tongue is designed to sense. Whether a sweet food is full-calorie, low-cal, or no-cal, when the brain senses the sweet taste, it assumes sugar is coming in and releases the chemicals and hormones for processing sugar. The result is a potentially compromised ability to release fat from the fat cells (recall step 1 of the process for fat burning). Ingesting sweet foods inhibits fat burning, compromising a key component of getting lean to show off your abs.

When to Eat

Remember, your goal is to reduce body fat through a three-step process and to maintain or build muscle. All the information in this book is presented with this goal in mind. In that spirit, consider three guidelines on when to eat:

1. **Never, ever skip breakfast.** If you skip breakfast, you will be one meal behind all day long. Your metabolism will have a hard time catching up. As chapter 2 discusses, your metabolism is like a campfire. Skipping breakfast forces your body to make do with less than what it needs. It slows down and clings to body fat, which makes it harder for you to get the abs you want. You should eat breakfast as soon as possible after waking up. If your last meal or snack was at 9 p.m. the night before and you wake up at 7 a.m. the next morning, you've already gone 10 hours without food! Your first meal,

quite literally, breaks the fast from the night before. If you're practicing the workouts in this book and proper nutrition, your metabolism will be revved up and asking you for breakfast as soon as you wake up.

2. **Always eat as soon as possible after a workout.** After you complete your workout, consume a meal containing protein and carbohydrate as soon as possible. A meal of two-thirds carbohydrate and one-third protein is on the right track. If you have a sweet tooth, this is the only safe time to indulge it. After a workout, your muscles are depleted of stored carbohydrate. Refueling quickly speeds their recovery and aids protein delivery for their repair, and it keeps you feeling energized after your training session.

3. **Eat every two to four hours.** Do you know someone who only eats once or twice per day? Most likely, this person's body is not in great shape. Although snakes eat a massive meal (an entire rodent!) before curling up under a rock to digest for several days, we are not snakes. We are humans whose bodies function best when fed regular meals every two to four hours. The only people who function when eating only once or twice per day are the ones who have been doing it for so long that their bodies have adapted by making negative changes that are often quite visible in their physique. This adaptation is never optimal for humans and is always the result of conditioning. If you are challenging your body appropriately with exercise, you'll naturally feel the urge to eat every two to four hours. Dr. John Berardi has a nice saying that illustrates how to spread calories throughout the meals in a day: "Eat like a king in the morning, a queen at lunch, and a pauper the rest of the day." This means you should eat your biggest meal first and then consume progressively smaller meals as you go through the day.

Basic Rules for Healthy Eating

The gray areas in nutrition have to do with the complexity of human biology, the chemical composition of foods, your tastes and preferences, and the genes that you inherited from your parents. However, you can follow a few specific rules that are organized here into two handy lists. If your goal is optimum fitness and great abs, never do the things on the first list and always do the things on the second list.

The Never List

This list includes the behaviors that are the most destructive to the goal of great abs. Note that this list plays a little bit with the word *never*. You don't have to be

MYTHS AND MISCONCEPTIONS

MYTH: You should never eat after a certain hour of the day.

REALITY: It's fine to eat a couple of hours before your bedtime.

The advice to never eat after a certain hour of the day is utter nonsense. If you stop eating at 6 p.m., but you don't go to sleep until midnight, you're going to feel hungry for hours, wrecking your results and metabolism. The correct approach is to eat for the last time one or two hours before your bedtime.

absolutely perfect on these concepts, but you do need to follow them the majority of the time. Never drink your calories, never skip meals (particularly breakfast), never eat any food that is deep-fried, never eat grains at night, never eat sugar except after a workout, and never eat any food with trans fat (hydrogenated oils).

Never Drink Calories

If you drink a lot of your calories from fruit juices, soda, milk, or the 700-calorie latte from the coffee shop, you will find it nearly impossible to get great abs. Since liquids don't fill up your stomach like solid foods do, you won't feel as though you've consumed very many calories. Except for milk (either from cow, soy, or nuts), most caloric beverages are nutritionally empty, offering little else but the sugar and fat they load into your body. Milk can be used for smoothies after your workout.

The only beverages that must be part of your daily drinking routines are water, coffee, and tea. Although many people mistakenly believe that coffee and tea dehydrate you, they do not cause you to eliminate more than the water it took to brew them. Fruit juices are not health food. If you want fruit, eat it. Juices simply concentrate the sugars. Freshly-squeezed orange juice is made up of anywhere between 6 and 12 oranges. Would you ever eat that many oranges in one sitting? Alcohol contains the simplest form of sugar and needs to be consumed accordingly. Of course, you can have an alcoholic drink with friends once in a while, but if you want great abs, you will only choose this beverage occasionally.

Never Skip Meals

Skipping breakfast is a mortal sin for this program and skipping other meals is not much better. Eat every two to four hours to fuel the fires of metabolism. If you don't eat regularly, you compromise results by forcing your body to live on less. In doing so, you alter metabolic hormones and force your body to choose between survival and appearance. When faced with these two options, your body will pick survival every time. Your biology is more resilient than all of your willpower. If you force your body to run on limited fuel, it will shift things around to keep you alive at the expense of your appearance.

Suppose you owned two cars. One is a monstrous, gas-guzzling, sport-utility vehicle and the other is a fuel-efficient model that gets a high number of miles per gallon. If there were a sudden fuel shortage, you would get rid of the gas-guzzler first, right? The same thing happens in your body when you start skipping meals. Fat is a very efficient and abundant source of fuel, and as a bonus, it requires very little energy for storage. Muscle, on the other hand, is very needy when it comes to calories. It uses a lot of calories just to keep itself around and to produce strength and power. In essence, the fuel cost of muscle is high. If you force your body into starvation mode, it must choose between muscle and fat. It begins to get rid of the gas guzzler (muscle and stored carbohydrate) but hangs on to fat. This phenomenon dupes people into believing that quick fixes work (see the sidebar on page 31). The human body has been using fat stores to prevent starvation in times of scarcity for millennia, so it has gotten very good at storing fat in preparation for the next famine. Your body doesn't know that you have an abundant food supply that you are simply not eating.

Never Eat Fried Foods

This one is a no-brainer. If it's deep-fried, it has no business going in your mouth. This isn't really a surprise, is it? If you want a healthy body and great abs, take anything dipped in a deep fryer off your menu.

MYTHS AND MISCONCEPTIONS

MYTH: Fasting, detox, and cleansing routines cut fat fast.

REALITY: Santa Claus isn't real, either.

Currently enjoying extensive promotion by celebrities and unscrupulous health gurus, the gimmicks of fasting, detox, and cleansing routines promise fat loss, better health, and, best of all, quick results. These invalid protocols can derail your fitness goals, compromise your metabolism, make you irritable, and damage your organs. These programs never adequately explain why toxins have been left behind by your liver or how they cleanse your colon. Your liver has been removing toxins just fine since the day you were born. Don't be fooled. Fasting will make you lose water (and a little fat), which will wreck your mood, and cleansing routines are fairy tales.

The smart approach is to limit your intake of toxins year-round rather than to follow an extreme detox ritual for several days before resuming a toxic diet for the rest of the year. If human beings were so precious, fragile, and delicate that we needed weird rituals to detoxify us, we'd have died out a long time ago. Don't be distracted by the false promises, intellectual sloppiness, and make-believe science of these magical routines for losing fat or weight. Feed your body what it needs, develop it through training, and maintain high performance.

Never Consume Sugar and Grains at Night

Sugar and grains are calorie-dense, action-packed foods that are the body's rocket fuel (recall the fuel sources from chapter 2). Why would you give your body rocket fuel when you'll be winding down and heading off to sleep soon? One exception exists to this rule: If your schedule dictates that you work out at night, you can safely consume complex carbohydrate and, if you're having a craving, even a little sugar right after your workout.

Never Eat Trans Fat

The good news is that most foods with trans fat are those that anyone seeking great abs would avoid anyway, such as doughnuts, cupcakes, cakes, cookies, candy, and commercial baked goods. However, trans fat also lurks in apparently healthy products like protein powders and bars. Eating trans fat is a surefire way to wreck your gut and your health. Remember, the U.S. government has not yet shown the courage to ban them, so it's your responsibility to read labels carefully. A lot of baked goods that are commercially available, such as a scone in the case at the coffee shop, also contain trans fat.

The Always List

This list includes the behaviors that are the most beneficial to the goal of great abs. As before, this list plays with the word *always*. You don't have to be absolutely perfect on these guidelines, but you do need to follow them the majority of the time if you want great abs. Always consume vegetables and complete, lean protein every time you eat; always eat healthy fat and avoid unhealthy fat; always plan, prepare, and pack good foods for your day; and get over it and move on when you slip up.

Always Eat Veggies at Every Meal

So many varieties of vegetables exist with different tastes, textures, and colors that you can always find some that you like. If you don't like any veggies, you're not listening to your body. Hating all vegetables is a learned behavior that is not part of our genetic makeup. Veggies are full of great plant chemicals and other vitamins and minerals, and they are low in calories and high in bulk. This means that they are the carbohydrate sources with the lowest caloric density. They deliver large doses of essential nutrients and make you feel full without adding excessive calories to your daily intake. If you have some veggies with every meal (spinach with your eggs at breakfast, a salad for lunch or dinner, or some bell peppers, carrots, and celery to dip in hummus), your body will thank you for it on the inside and on the outside.

Always Eat Protein Every Time You Eat

Never snack on a banana alone. Every time you eat, you need to include some protein. Whether you're an omnivore or a vegetarian, have some lean meat, fish, low-fat dairy, eggs, tofu, quinoa, a veggie burger, or the occasional protein supplement.

Always Eat Healthy Fat

You might be shocked to learn that you'll feel best, train your best, recover your best, and as a result, look your best when consuming 20 to 30 percent of your calories from fat. Remember, you need a little saturated fat. Most oils, nuts, and even leaner cuts of meat contain some saturated fat. You don't need any additional saturated fat in your diet, so skip the butter, full-fat sour cream, full-fat cheeses, and marbled meats. Also, watch out for palm oils, which are overused by many companies in food processing and are almost exclusively saturated. It's easier than you might think to incorporate healthy fats into your eating plan. You can add an avocado to smoothies, have a handful of nuts for a snack, and eat fatty fish once or twice each week.

Always Plan, Prepare, and Pack Healthy Foods

When you are out of the house and you allow yourself to get hungry, you go after the quickest and easiest foods. These are almost never good choices. Whether you're eating lunch at work, out running errands, or just hanging out at home, have a plan for nutrition. It doesn't have to be complicated or gourmet, but it does need to be strategic.

To use this strategy, identify typical times during your week when you find yourself hungry and without a healthy option. Write down some healthy options that you could prepare ahead of time and take with you, then make a list of foods and go shopping. Next, choose one or two times each week to do your prep work. For example, you can prepare five or six salads at a time, doing all the chopping at once before assembling them in single-serving containers. During the week, all you need to do is to dress the salad before eating. Another healthy option for after your workout could be something as simple as apple slices and a sandwich of peanut butter (or another nut butter like almond) on whole-grain bread. Planning for the meals that commonly occur at times you know are difficult will help you stay on target for your goals by preventing ravenous hunger that drives you to make unwise food choices.

If You Slip Up, Get Over It and Move On

This is so important. When it comes to nutrition and exercise, we tend to be far too hard on ourselves. We mess up by eating something that we shouldn't or by missing a workout, and the next thing we know, we're in a tailspin that often leads to even worse choices. If we lived other parts of our lives with the same high standards, every time our car broke down, we'd push it off a cliff and get a

MYTHS AND MISCONCEPTIONS

MYTH: Good and bad foods don't exist.

REALITY: Oh, yes, they do!

Overly sensitive dietitians and touchy-feely food counselors try to sugarcoat the realities of nutrition, and as you now know, sugarcoating anything is a bad idea! Their motives are pure. So many people have food issues that they don't want to create more trouble by making definitive statements, but this practice keeps them from telling it like it is, even when the truth is obvious. If a food promotes health and fitness and provides the human body with what it needs to support life, it is a good food. If a food destroys health and fitness and gives the human body nothing it needs, it is a bad food.

Our bodies are hardy and strong enough that we don't drop dead from eating one cupcake, and we don't become superheroes by eating one salad. However, anything you eat is either adding to or subtracting from health, fitness, and vitality. For example, a deep-fried candy bar at a county or state fair is always a bad food. This is a simple statement of fact. Can you eat one and live to tell about it? Sure, but, by doing so, your body moved one (big) step in an unhealthy direction. You don't have to be perfect, you just have to choose good food the majority of the time.

new one. If we had a bad day at work, we'd quit and find a new job. One fight with your partner would lead to a breakup and a return to the dating scene. Give yourself the same freedom to make a nutrition mistake and move on without beating yourself up. The key is to learn from the mistake by developing a strategy, a plan of attack to avoid repeating the same mistake again. Next, move on. Get over it and keep going forward.

How to Enjoy Healthy Food

Lots of people think fitness experts eat nothing but bark and lawn clippings, but they could not be more wrong. They love to eat, but they also love their bodies and value health. We are meant to enjoy food, but our culture has come to use food as a reward. We've also been brainwashed about what tastes good and what it means to enjoy food. As a result, when I work with people who need to make changes in their nutrition, I frequently hear many of the same concerns. The following list outlines a few of the most common concerns:

- **Healthy food tastes boring.** Imagine a warm, bright, sunny day. You head outside to toss the ball around with friends. When you come back inside, the color in your vision is washed out and everything takes on a pale or greenish tinge. In a short while, your eyes recover their ability to perceive differences in color and brightness, and the world looks normal again. What does this have to do with healthy food? Your taste buds are just like your eyes, but they take longer to recover. If your taste buds have been routinely assaulted by sweet and salty junk foods with unnaturally strong flavors, they will not be able to detect the natural flavors in healthy food, thus creating the illusion that the food tastes bland. Once you let your taste buds recover their normal senses, the natural flavors in healthy foods can come out again. With taste buds that are finely tuned, you can taste the difference between green and red bell peppers.

- **I can't cook.** Then learn! Please stop making excuses. If you knew someone who just chuckled and threw their hands up with laughter while saying, "I don't know how to drive," you'd probably think that they were odd. You might even think that they should learn to drive because it is an essential skill. It's no different with cooking. Remember, our history is as hunter-gatherers. If you didn't know how to cook, you didn't survive. Knowing how to prepare a meal is an essential survival skill. Don't be intimidated. It's not as hard as you've possibly imagined it to be. You surely know someone who can show you the basics. You can also find introductory cooking classes to learn a few basic skills. The worst that can happen is that you make a mistake that you learn from.

- **I can't eat healthy food at restaurants.** This is a tough problem, since few restaurants cater exclusively to those seeking good nutrition. A waitress that I know who has lost a lot of weight offered this great, simple tip: Remember that it is your food! Don't be afraid to ask for modifications. Skip the butter or heavy sauce, ask for less oil in sautéed dishes, substitute mixed veggies for fries, and get sauces, dressing, and cheeses on the side. Most restaurants have at least one or two options for the health-conscious diner, and you can modify many of the rest.

- **Healthy food is too expensive.** Junk food is too cheap to make. Food has historically come from plants and animals, not from assembly lines. The advent of food manufacturing that uses low-quality, low-cost ingredients to make prepackaged foods that are worth very little should not be the standard by which we compare food prices. Working the soil, planting seeds, tending crops, harvesting them, and preparing them for transport and sale cannot be compared to manufacturing a cupcake. In life, you get what you pay for. Healthy food costs more than junk food that is unrealistically, artificially cheap. Furthermore, food companies want profits. If the profits were better for healthy food, they would promote and market it aggressively. The reality is that junk food, which is engineered to be addictive, is more profitable, so it gets promoted. Finally, you cannot simply consider the price when buying food. You must also consider the short-term and long-term implications for your health. Also, it's worth noting that you vote with your money with every purchase. Every consumer choice has an environmental impact, whether great or small.

Let's take a closer look at the issue of quality. You hear all the time that the key to weight loss is simple: Calories in must equal calories out. Many people think that all you have to do is eat less and exercise. In fact, not all calories are equal. This is like saying that all cars are the same. Cars, of course, come in different sizes and shapes, not to mention fuel economies. Humans are not bank accounts in which equal deposits and withdrawals equate to a balance of zero. Since we are alive, we react to various things differently.

As a short-term strategy, it's easy to lose weight by cutting your calories drastically low, even if you eat low-quality food. However, as soon as your body figures out what is happening, it puts hormones to work to stop the weight loss. Over time, junk food can make a mess of your health. Typically, hormones create all of your body's reactions and drive just about everything in your body. They control sleep, the building of muscle, fat loss, and many other biological processes. Imagine two identical twins with the same exercise program. One eats 2,500 calories per day of lean protein, whole grains, fruits, nuts, and vegetables, and the other eats 2,500 calories of table sugar. Wouldn't you suppose that the response of their bodies to this identical caloric intake would be far different? The hormonal response of the twin who ate sugar would be far different from that of the other one. Although this is an extreme example, chosen only to illustrate the concept, it should be obvious that quality of your calories makes a big difference in your body. Quantity does matter, but quality matters just as much.

Stripping away preferences, emotional issues, desires, or other subjective measures of the purpose and quality of food, we find that food is ultimately designed to provide your body with what it needs to move, repair damage, make new cells, and so on. We need to enjoy healthy food, and it should taste good so we will eat more of it. Here are a couple of helpful tips to help you enjoy healthy eating:

1. **Use herbs and spices.** This secret weapon brings out new and healthy flavors in simple dishes. At first, purchase some common dried herbs, such as basil, tarragon, rosemary, or any other herb you might recognize by name. Next, pick up some aromatic spices (many of which have many health benefits in addition to added flavor) like turmeric or cumin. After you've gotten a sense of the flavors of dried herbs, you can try buying fresh herbs or even growing your own. Chopping them up and adding them to eggs, a chicken breast, or a soup is a great way to add flavor.

2. **Make a better salad.** Salads got a bad rap from all the poor versions that have been served for so long. Skip the iceberg lettuce. You can buy premixed, prewashed salad greens, and then add chopped veggies that you know you like. Over time, you can try a new vegetable or two. For example, fennel (similar to celery) makes a novel, interesting addition. Next, to keep salads from getting too boring, turn up the interest factor and nutritional quality. Try adding some pumpkin seeds, or any other nut you like, for added protein and healthy fat. Try adding some herbs (either dried or fresh). For an added dash of flavor, use a small amount of a strongly flavored cheese like feta. Sprinkle some ground flax seeds on for added omega-3 fat and fiber. The only dressing you'll ever need is a high-quality olive oil with some balsamic vinegar. You can add canned tuna, salmon, or a grilled chicken breast for some high-quality protein.

Head Check: What's Important to You?

Often, when I'm giving clients guidance about making better food choices, they say something like, "You mean I can't have chicken wings? You've got to live once in a while!" With all that life offers and all there is to see, do, and experience in the world, how can someone's idea of getting the most out of life be eating chicken wings? It's not wrong to think like this, but doing so will prevent you from achieving the body you want. It will certainly not lead to great abs. If unhealthy food has a higher value for you than a well-sculpted midsection, your expectations need to change. Just about everything in life is a choice, and great abs are no different.

Putting It Into Practice

It can be difficult make the right choices with food and put them into practice in the real world, but remember this to stay on track:

Your body builds itself from your habits.

What you do most of the time will determine the type of body you walk around in. This doesn't mean that eating some cake at your birthday party or a few of Grandma's holiday cookies will turn you into an elephant overnight. However, it also doesn't mean you can have a few pieces of chocolate every day or beer and hot wings three nights a week and still have great abs. Your habits are what your body recognizes as normal. If you spend 90 percent of your diet on the good stuff, your body will be satisfied with the right amounts of healthy fat, carbohydrate, protein, vitamins, and minerals. So when you eat the occasional food that isn't part of your good habits, your body will recognize it as abnormal and will get rid of most of it.

As you read through this chapter, you were asked to note the parts that jumped out as the most relevant to you. This is where you begin. By now, you know that your aim is to eliminate that which interrupts any of the three steps of fat loss, and to do more to promote these steps. To help you take this information into your daily life, you're going to build a prioritized list of nutrition changes, which will help you change your habits systematically so you don't feel overwhelmed by doing too much at once. It can be difficult to alter multiple habits at once, so prioritize the hardest things first to ensure the greatest impact. Keep in mind that the faster you do what you need, the faster you will get great abs.

For example, if you're currently not eating breakfast or eating vegetables, and you're stopping for fast food every other day; drinking one or two sodas every day; eating huge dinners with lots of bread, pasta, or potatoes; and having chicken wings and a few beers several times a week at happy hour, where do you begin? It might be too much of a shock to fix all this at once. Prioritize your list of nutrition changes in the following way:

1. Eat breakfast every day and reduce your portion sizes, especially of the carbohydrate, at dinner.

2. Go to happy hour only once per week and use your free evenings for grocery shopping and meal planning.

3. Drink sodas only once every other day and increase water intake.

4. Begin adding vegetables to meals: Try salad with grilled chicken and seeds at lunch and carrots and celery with hummus for a snack. Try cooking one new vegetable per week.

5. Replace all white breads and flour products with whole-grain ones.

If I were working with you one on one, I might suggest trying only item 1 for one or two weeks. This item solves the problems of skipping breakfast and eating too much of the wrong things at dinner. (Overeating at dinner is often a result of skipping breakfast.) If you're feeling ambitious, you might try items 1 and 2 right away. Either way, once these changes become a part of your normal routine, simply move to the next item on the list. Do that one for a few weeks until it also feels normal, then move to the next item on the list. This process simply repeats for a lifetime, so you're always doing things a little bit better as you go on.

I'll give you a personal example. When I was in my early 20s, my eating habits were pretty bad. Among other bad nutrition habits, I was drinking two or three regular sodas per day. When I committed to getting healthier, I got down to one soda per day with lunch. It's been many years since then. At the time, reducing my soda intake to one per day was a big accomplishment. However, if I were still at that point today, it would be a disaster, given the changes I've accumulated over the years. See how this works? If I had sworn off sodas immediately when I was used to drinking two or three per day, I probably couldn't have handled it. By making the changes at a rate that I could handle, the result was much better and more permanent. I've been able to sustain the changes and build on them. Now, I drink maybe one soda per year, if that.

Now it's your turn. Take out a pen and paper, make a task list in your planner, write yourself a list in your smartphone, or write them on a sticky note and put it on your bathroom mirror. Begin making your numbered, prioritized list of nutrition changes that will propel you to your best body and best abs ever. You can work your way through the list at a pace that is appropriate for you. Remember, the faster you make the changes you need to your daily habits, the faster your body will start to look and feel its best. Your body builds itself from your habits, whether good or bad.

PART II

Exercises for Chiseled Abs

Working Toward the Washboard

As chapter 1 discusses, in order to get great outer abs, you need to fire up the inner abs. Recall the analogy of the best winter coat. Now it's time to put on the layers underneath the coat so you can go out and play. The exercises here make up stage 1 (see chapter 8 for more details) of developing great abs. The amazing thing about these exercises is how hard your abs will work by preventing and controlling movement. Many of them involve initiating muscle tension and holding it to sustain a body position. These deceptively simple exercises are designed to maximize development of your inner and outer abs by torching your muscles. What could be better than great abs inside and out?

Great abs can be as simple as a game of rock, paper, scissors. The exercises in this chapter make up the Rock phase of your *Abs Revealed* workouts. These essential exercises all feature turning on certain muscles, creating tension, and preventing movement or loss of tension once the proper position is obtained. This process helps you switch on your inner abs in order to move the outer ones. The exercises from pages 44 to 52 provide either stability or mobility in your abs. They give you the tools you need to work toward the washboard. Since they don't require equipment, you can do them anywhere, anytime!

The first four exercises help you establish an awareness of your inner abs. The inner abs eventually switch on automatically so you should not need to consciously activate them for long. These four exercises provide the foundational technique to allow you to successfully perform the others exercises in this chapter. Movement is introduced in these exercises, and they are awesome additions to your training. Other exercises use two great pieces of equipment, a stability ball and the TRX, to train the abs. For the stability ball exercises, you can use a regular stability ball or if you have a Ballast ball from BOSU, you can use it to add a new level of challenge for many of the stability ball exercises in this book. The Ballast ball is a stability ball filled with gravel-like material that adds additional and shifting weight to your workout. The TRX is easily the best piece of fitness equipment to

Rehab for Exercise Names

If you read anything in the popular media about exercise, you'll easily see that all too often, exercise names are pointless and confusing. Many trainers add to the problem by continuing to use these names. Have you ever heard of an exercise called a burpee? It sounds like something you do after a large meal. The term for the exercise that is far more accurate and meaningful is a squat thrust, which at least tells you something about what you might be doing.

Consider the following exercise names that are commonly used: Bulgarian split squat, Romanian deadlift, Turkish get-up, and Russian twist. Does every country in Eastern Europe have its own exercise? These names tell you nothing about the actual exercise movement. The foolishness in exercise names isn't limited to geography. Some people use the name of another person (Arnold press, for example) for an exercise. Exercise names should describe the movement and communicate useful information. You won't find any childish, nonsensical exercise names in this text. An exception to this rule is with names like plank that have such a common frame of reference that most people know what they are even if they've never done them.

come out recently. The TRX is a rigid nylon strap that anchors to a fixed point. It allows you to perform a wide range of unique body weight exercises by placing your hands or feet in it and keeping the other end of your body on the ground. (See the Using the TRX section.) The TRX is highly portable; can be used easily at the gym, at home, or on vacation; and ignites your abs in nearly every exercise. For additional information on the equipment and exercises used throughout *Abs Revealed*, visit www.AbsRevealed.com.

If you're just beginning your journey to a stellar six-pack, consider this word of caution: Exercises that work the lower abs are often so demanding that even one repetition is impossible. What can you do if your lower abs are weak, but the exercises you need to strengthen them are insanely difficult? Try the reverse crunch with hand targets on page 48. You can use this simple technique to hit your lower abs hard. If you find the other exercises for the lower abs too challenging, don't give up. If you can even do three great reps, you'll soon manage four. Don't cheat in order to do more reps. Three reps with excellent technique will do more for you than 12 reps with bad technique. The actual programming for these exercises is revealed in chapter 8.

Type of exercise	Page number
Floor	44
Stability ball	53
TRX	62

Draw-Ins, Braces, and Planks

Sit-ups used to rule the earth. Soon crunches rose to the top of the food chain and sit-ups were shunned. Not long after, crunches became outdated, especially the method of performing hundreds of crunches because it can lead to spinal disc injuries. Next, planks were all the rage. More recently, the concepts of an abdominal draw-in and an abdominal brace have enjoyed popularity. They have received the inevitable criticism that follows whenever any single approach is deemed the be-all and end-all of abdominal training. Once again, the fundamental mistake is the need to classify elements as either right or wrong. In reality, any of the preceding exercises can be useful, depending on your goals and abilities.

As you gain a better understanding of how your body works, you don't have to throw out everything that came before. Planks are a great gateway exercise, or a stepping-stone to other exercises. They are great for developing stability in the inner abs, but they don't feel natural. We are creatures who need to move! When we move, our abs alternate rapidly between on and off muscle actions to allow us to create and control movement. Draw-ins also develop your ability to activate and contract the inner abs, allowing them to stay stable while the outer abs do their thing. Braces are a step up. They are more appropriate for weight-training activities, since they involve tightening and contracting both the inner and outer abs.

Using the TRX

When the TRX is freely swinging, it moves back to the neutral point underneath the anchor. This movement helps you create different levels of resistance by changing your starting position for exercises performed with your heels or toes in the foot cradles. For this type of exercise, start in the neutral position, letting your feet hang directly under the anchor point (see figure 4.1). In general, when you move your body toward the neutral point so that your feet move to the other side of the neutral position (see figure 4.2), the resistance decreases. This is because your body and the TRX will both move in the same direction (toward the neutral point). Similarly, when you move your body and feet farther away from the neutral point on your side of the neutral point (see figure 4.3), resistance increases because your body and the TRX are moving in opposite directions during the exercise. Your body will move farther away from the neutral point as the TRX tries to move toward it.

FIGURE 4.1   **Neutral starting position.**

FIGURE 4.2   **Starting position for less resistance.**

FIGURE 4.3   **Starting position for more resistance.**

▶ **POSITION**

Lie on your back, bend your knees, and place your feet flat on the floor.

▶ **TECHNIQUE**

1. Use your fingers to find your hip bones. Move your hands toward each other along the waistline. Stop when you feel the soft area before the rectus abdominis muscle (main abdominal muscle). This area is located somewhere between your hip bones and your navel.
2. Make the soft area hard by activating the deepest muscles of the inner abs. Avoid tightening the outer abs.

▶ **PERFORMANCE TIPS**

Avoid a full, high-intensity contraction, which will activate the muscles of the outer abs. Imagine the soft area under your fingers slowly getting harder. When you can just feel the tension forming in this area, stop contracting the muscle. Adding intensity to the contraction will activate the outer muscles. You shouldn't feel like you're working very hard on this exercise. Make sure you can activate the deepest layers of abdominal muscle. This will eventually happen automatically. Practice makes automatic for this type of exercise.

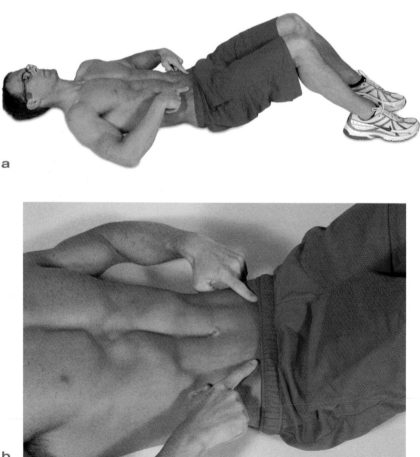

a

b

▶ **POSITION**

Lie on your back, bend your knees, and place your feet flat on the floor.

▶ **TECHNIQUE**

1. Locate your hip bones with your fingers. Move your hands together along your waistline. Stop when you get to the soft area before the rectus abdominis muscle (main ab muscle).

2. Harden this area by activating the deepest muscles of your inner abs while simultaneously tightening your outer abs.

▶ **PERFORMANCE TIPS**

Imagine you are back in grade school and you have just challenged a friend to hit you in the abs. Brace yourself as if anticipating a blow.

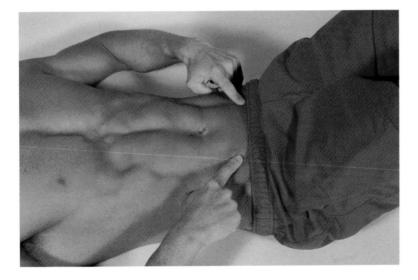

▶ POSITION

Lie facedown, propping yourself up with your elbows. Hold your forearms flat and tuck your toes under.

▶ TECHNIQUE

1. Brace your abs and begin to lift your hips off the floor.
2. As you lift your hips, imagine that you are driving your elbows into the ground.

▶ PERFORMANCE TIPS

In the final position, your hips should be aligned with your shoulders and ankles. Keep your shoulders over your elbows.

▶ POSITION

Lie on your side and prop yourself up with your elbow. Your elbow should be positioned directly under your shoulder. All points along your body line should be straight, from the top of your head to your feet.

▶ TECHNIQUE

1. Brace your abs and begin lifting your hips off the floor.

2. As you lift your hips, imagine driving your elbow into the ground.

▶ PERFORMANCE TIPS

In the final position, your hips should be lined up with your shoulders and ankles. Be sure that you do not bend at the hips. Keep your shoulders aligned vertically over your bottom elbow, and keep your bottom shoulder away from your ear on the same side.

a

b

Reverse Crunch With Hand Targets

▶ POSITION

Lie on your back with your hips and knees fully flexed. You are essentially curling into a ball without holding your legs in place. Bend your elbows, angle your hands toward your legs, position your palms a few inches from your knees, and rest the backs of your upper arms on the floor.

▶ TECHNIQUE

1. Brace your abs and lift your hips in (toward your shoulders) and up, focusing more on inward than upward movement. The movement brings your knees toward your hands (the targets).

2. Continue pulling your hips in and up with your abs until your knees gently touch your palms. Your hips and the lowermost part of your spine will lose contact with the floor.

3. Once your knees have touched your palms, return to the starting position gently and with control. Avoid losing tension in the abs at the end of the movement.

▶ PERFORMANCE TIPS

Imagine a rope attached to the bottom of your pelvis is running through your torso just in front of your spine. Perform the exercise by pulling this imaginary rope along its length through your torso. Movement in this exercise is minimal, but it will work your lower abs very hard. Even so, anyone can perform this exercise. At the end of the movement, be especially careful to keep your thighs from swinging forward. Avoid opening the space between your thighs and torso.

a

b

▶ POSITION

Lie on your back and raise your legs and arms into the air. Flex your knees to 90 degrees and position your thighs and arms perpendicular to the floor. Your shins and torso should be parallel to the floor.

▶ TECHNIQUE

1. Brace your abs. As you lower one arm over your head toward the floor, begin to straighten the opposite leg. The arm and leg will both move away from your torso in opposite directions. Use your abs to protect your spine during movement.

2. In the final position, your leg is straight. Your arm and leg should be parallel to the floor.

3. Return to the starting position and repeat with the other arm and leg.

▶ PERFORMANCE TIPS

Your lower back should be neither flat nor excessively arched. Maintain a neutral position of the lower spine by using your abs to move your arms and legs.

a

b

Harder-Than-It-Looks (HTIL) Crunch

▶ **POSITION**

Lie down on your back, flex your knees, and place your feet flat on the floor. Form one hand into a fist and position it under your chin, resting your pinky finger under your chin and your thumb and forefinger against the upper part of your chest. Gently position your other hand behind your neck.

▶ **TECHNIQUE**

1. First, move your ribs closer to your hips.
2. Continue the movement by lifting your shoulder blades off the floor as you would for a normal crunch.
3. Return to the starting position.

▶ **PERFORMANCE TIPS**

You should complete the crunch before you see any signs of movement in your body. This exercise helps you eliminate any compensating or cheating that you may be unconsciously doing while performing crunches. It breaks the crunch into segmented actions so you can master each part.

a

b

▶ POSITION

Lie on your back, flex your knees, and place your feet flat on the floor. Bring your torso off the floor by either performing a crunch or pulling yourself up to a seated position. Keep your spine long as you hold the backs of your thighs and sit up.

▶ TECHNIQUE

1. Slowly lower your torso back toward the ground, keeping your spine long and your torso open as long as you can.

2. When you can no longer hold your torso straight, allow your spine to curl. Lower your back to the floor and return to the starting position of the crunch with control.

▶ PERFORMANCE TIPS

This exercise emphasizes control. Your aim is to keep your spine long and straight for as long as possible while intentionally moving toward the floor. Negative crunches create significant muscle tension. They are a surefire way to hit all your ab muscles hard.

a

b

Quadruped Draw-In With Arm and Leg Movement (Bird Dog)

▶ **POSITION**

Get on the floor on all fours, aligning your shoulders over your hands and your hips over your knees.

▶ **TECHNIQUE**

1. Perform a draw-in (see page 44) as described for the supine position. However, the prone position adds difficulty.

2. While maintaining a neutral spine position, slowly extend one arm in front of you. At the same time, slowly extend the opposite leg straight out behind you. The arm and leg should move away from your torso in opposite directions. Movement should originate in your shoulder and your glutes as you maintain a rock-solid position with your abs.

3. Return your arm and leg to the starting position and repeat with the opposite arm and leg.

▶ **PERFORMANCE TIPS**

This exercise is not hard to do; it's just hard to do well! Moving your arm and leg with total abdominal stability is surprisingly challenging because many of us unconsciously compensate. Your shoulder or hip joint should not lift as your arm and leg move, which indicates that the spine and abs are extending. Your arm and your leg will move, but the shoulder and hip joint stay relatively stable. In this case, your spine creates the movement, not your shoulder and hip joints.

a

b

▶ POSITION

Get into a push-up position with your legs on the ball. Position the ball on your thighs just above your knees. Keep your knees flexed.

▶ TECHNIQUE

1. Drive the tops of your thighs into the ball while bracing your abs.
2. Keep your shoulders aligned over your hands while you roll the ball toward your head.
3. Stop the movement just before your knees are vertically aligned with your hips and return to the start position.

▶ PERFORMANCE TIPS

Try to "pop the ball" with your knees by driving them into the ball using your abs. Your hips will lift because you are pressing your legs into the ball. If you perform this exercise by lifting your hips instead of pushing your legs into the ball, it will feel very easy and you will not feel much effort from your abs.

a   b

Side Plank on Stability Ball

▶ POSITION

Lie on your side and prop yourself up with your elbow, placing it directly under your shoulder. All points of your body should be aligned, from the top of your head to your feet. The ball is positioned between your feet and ankles. Placing the ball between your feet changes the process of the basic side plank in two ways: It introduces an element of instability in your lower extremities and shifts body weight to your upper extremities for more loading.

▶ TECHNIQUE

1. Brace your abs and lift your hips off the floor into a straight line with your shoulders and ankles. Extend your top arm up.

2. As you lift your hips, imagine driving your elbow into the ground.

▶ PERFORMANCE TIPS

Be sure that you don't flex your hips or bend at the waist. Keep your shoulders aligned vertically over your bottom elbow and keep your bottom shoulder away from your ear on that side. Experiment with applying different amounts of pressure on the ball with your legs to change the intensity of the exercise.

a

b

▶ POSITION

Lie on your back and flex your hips and knees to form a 90-degree angle. Position your legs on the ball so that the back of your thighs and calves are touching it. Hold your arms straight by your sides with your palms open and turned down.

▶ TECHNIQUE

1. Dig your heels into the ball and squeeze it into the back of your thighs. Next, lift the ball off the floor slightly. This is the starting position.

2. Use your lower abs to lift your hips in and up.

3. Return your hips to the floor and the ball to the starting position (hovering just above the floor).

▶ PERFORMANCE TIPS

The ball should not touch the floor until the set is finished. Perform this exercise by lifting your hips rather than by flexing them. Your hips move first and your legs come along for the ride. You'll know you're doing it properly if your lower abs tire quickly! If it feels too easy, check your movement. If your knees move in toward your chest before your hips move, you are using the momentum of moving your thighs to lift your hips rather than doing it with your abs.

If you are wearing shorts, the tacky surface of the ball should firmly grip the skin on the back of your thighs, holding it in place while you perform the movement. If you are wearing pants, the ball may slip against the back of your thighs. In this case, simply open your legs a little wider and grip the ball slightly with the inside of your heels.

a

b

Semi-Vise Crunch With Stability Ball

▶ POSITION

Lie on your back and straighten out your legs on the floor. Lifting one leg in the air slightly, place the ball on the thigh just above the knee. Gently hold it in place with the arm on the same side as the elevated leg by placing your open palm on the front of the ball.

▶ TECHNIQUE

1. Use your abs to simultaneously lift the leg that is under the ball and your upper torso from the floor. Maintain tension on the ball with your hand and keep your arm straight.

2. Continue raising your leg and your torso. The ball will naturally roll up your leg, finishing somewhere below your knee, depending on your strength and range of motion.

3. While maintaining control, slowly return to the starting position. Lower your leg almost all the way to the floor. Your shoulder blades may lightly tap the floor.

▶ PERFORMANCE TIPS

Your arm and leg form a vise that holds the ball in place on one side of your body. You can control the intensity of the contraction in your abs by changing how hard you press your hand and leg against the ball and toward one another. Remember to keep your arm straight throughout the entire movement. Your leg and shoulder blades should not fully rest on the floor until you have completed the set.

a

b

▶ POSITION

Lie on your back and place your legs straight on the floor. Position the ball over both of your thighs, halfway between your knees and hips. Keep your arms straight and your palms open. Since the bottom of the ball rests on your thighs, place your hands on the front of the ball.

▶ TECHNIQUE

1. Keeping your arms straight, simultaneously lift your legs and your upper torso from the floor.

2. Continue raising your legs and your torso higher. The ball will naturally roll up your legs, finishing somewhere below your knees, depending on your strength and range of motion.

3. Maintaining control, slowly return to the starting position by lowering your legs almost all the way to the floor. Allow your shoulder blades to lightly tap the floor.

▶ PERFORMANCE TIPS

Your arms and legs essentially form a vise that holds the ball in place. Maintain straight arms throughout the entire movement. The ball moves with your torso as your arms transfer their movement to the ball. Control the intensity of the contraction in your abs by varying how hard you press your hands and legs against the ball and toward one another. Avoid fully resting your legs and shoulder blades on the floor until the completion of the set.

a

b

▶ **POSITION**

Lie on your back and place your legs straight on the floor. Position the ball over both of your thighs, halfway between your knees and hips. Keep your arms straight and your palms open. Since the bottom of the ball rests on your thighs, place your hands on the front of the ball.

▶ **TECHNIQUE**

1. Keeping your arms straight, simultaneously lift your legs and your upper torso off the floor.

2. Continue raising both your legs and your torso. The ball will naturally roll up your legs, finishing somewhere below your knees, depending on your strength and range of motion.

3. At the end of the movement, roll the ball around your legs while holding the position at the top. Roll the ball once to the left and once to the right before returning it to the middle.

4. With control, slowly return to the starting position by lowering your legs almost all the way to the floor. Your shoulder blades may lightly tap the floor.

▶ **PERFORMANCE TIPS**

Your arms and legs form a vise that holds the ball in place. Keep your arms straight throughout the entire movement. You can control the intensity of the contraction in your abs by changing how hard you press your hands and legs against the ball and toward one another. As you roll the ball around your legs, try to keep them as still as possible. In other words, you're moving the ball around your legs rather than moving your legs around the ball. Your legs and shoulder blades should not fully rest on the floor until you have completed the set.

a   b

▶ POSITION

Lie on your back and flex your hips and knees to a 90-degree angle. Your thighs should be perpendicular to the floor and your shins should be parallel to the floor. Place the ball on your shins. The focus of this tricky exercise is balancing the ball while maintaining the position of your hips and lower back. Your arms should be straight by your sides with your palms open and turned down. Your lower back is neutral (neither flat nor arched), creating a small amount of space between your lower back and the floor.

▶ TECHNIQUE

1. Brace your abs to prepare for the movement, and then begin extending your knees, which lowers your shins. Concentrate on keeping your shins parallel to the floor as you protect the position of your lower spine and hips. Essentially, this position should not change as your legs move.

2. Move slowly until you sense you have reached the limit of your control. This occurs when you cannot straighten your knees and lower your legs without losing control of your hips and lower back. Once you have reached this point, return to the starting position.

▶ PERFORMANCE TIPS

As your control gets stronger over time, you'll be able to lower the legs more, but don't rush it! Control must come first, keeping the inner abs in charge of the movement so that the outer abs can do the heavy lifting. Use the range of motion of your abs while maintaining spinal stability to get stronger and better at this exercise.

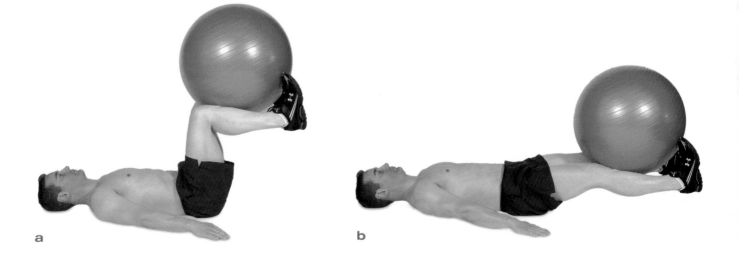

a   b

Plank With Elbows on Stability Ball

▶ **POSITION**

To begin, face the stability ball. Bend your elbows and place your forearms flat on the ball, then lean on it, facing down. Your legs should be extended and your toes should be tucked under on the floor. Your chest or torso should make contact with the ball.

▶ **TECHNIQUE**

1. Brace your abs and lift your hips. At the same time, press your elbows into the ball to lift your chest and torso up.

2. As you hold the position, be sure your hips are in a straight line with your shoulders and ankles.

▶ **PERFORMANCE TIPS**

The technique is similar to that of the plank exercise. Using the ball under your upper body creates a greater demand for stability, which activates your inner and outer abs.

▶ **VARIATION**

For a challenging variation, rock from front to back while holding the position. Note how the point of greatest intensity in your abs moves as you change position.

a

b

▶ **POSITION**

Begin by kneeling in front of the ball and placing your torso against it. Roll forward and lower your forearms to the floor. Walk your forearms farther out until your shins are on top of the ball.

▶ **TECHNIQUE**

1. Once you finish getting into position, you're already doing the exercise!
2. As in other plank exercises, hold the position that places your hips in a straight line with your shoulders and ankles.

▶ **PERFORMANCE TIPS**

Your inner and outer abs must work together to keep you stable. Elevating your legs on the ball also adds additional load to your upper body, making it more difficult to hold the position with your abs and shoulders.

▶ **VARIATION**

For a challenging variation, rock from front to back while holding the hip position. Note how the point of greatest intensity in your abs moves as you change position.

a

b

▶ **POSITION**

Lie on your back with your head under the anchor point. Holding your arms straight and angled out to the side, press your open palms into the handles. Lift both legs straight up so that they are directly or nearly over your hips.

▶ **TECHNIQUE**

1. Begin lowering both legs in a straight line toward the floor. As your legs move closer to the floor, the position of your hips and lower back should not change.

2. Lower your legs as far as possible without losing control of your hips and lower back, moving slowly so that you can sense when you are reaching your limit of control.

3. Return to the starting position.

▶ **PERFORMANCE TIPS**

Keep your arms straight and apply a strong downward force through the palms of your hands throughout the movement. As you lower your legs toward the floor, move slowly enough that you have time to sense and react to the increasing challenge for your inner and outer abs.

a

b

▶ POSITION

Lie on your back with your head under the anchor point. Holding your arms straight and angled out to the side, press your open palms into the handles. Your knees should be bent and your feet should be flat on the floor. (*Resisted* means that the TRX adds to the resistance. If it were moving freely, it would move toward you during the exercise.)

▶ TECHNIQUE

1. Roll up, keeping your arms straight and applying consistent downward force to the handles. Stop when your shoulders are almost over your hips.

2. Return to the starting position with control, maintaining the downward force on the handles.

▶ PERFORMANCE TIPS

To keep tension in your abs between reps, lower yourself down until you feel your shoulder blades tap the floor. If you notice your ribs popping up at the end of the movement, you're relaxing the abs.

a   b

▶ POSITION

Sit with your legs straight, positioning your feet directly under the anchor point of the TRX. Place your heels in the foot cradles and lie down on your back, then lift your arms until they are straight and perpendicular to the floor.

▶ TECHNIQUE

1. Anchor your heels in the foot cradles and lift your torso off the floor.
2. As you approach the top of the movement, lengthen your spine and come forward until your shoulders are over your hips and your arms are over your head.
3. Return to the starting position with control.

▶ PERFORMANCE TIPS

As you rise, lift your torso through your arms. This keeps your arms perpendicular to the floor throughout the exercise, whether they are over your chest (at the beginning) or next to your head (at the end). Securing your heels in the foot cradles keeps the hip flexors from dominating the movement and puts more emphasis on your abs.

STARTING POSITION

TORSO LIFTS THROUGH ARMS

FINISHING POSITION

Assisted Roll-Up With TRX

▶ POSITION

Lie on your back with your knees slightly bent and your feet under the anchor point of the TRX. Holding your arms straight and angled out to the side, press your open palms into the handles. Your knees should be bent and your feet should be flat on the floor. (*Assisted* means that the TRX helps you slightly. If it were moving freely, it would move with you during the exercise.)

▶ TECHNIQUE

1. Roll up, keeping your arms straight and applying consistent downward force to the handles. Stop when your shoulders are almost over your hips.
2. Return to the starting position with control, maintaining downward force on the handles.

▶ PERFORMANCE TIPS

To keep tension in your abs between reps, lower yourself down until you feel your shoulder blades tap the floor. If you notice your ribs popping up at the end of the movement, you're relaxing your abs. Avoid bending your elbows or pulling with your arms. To prevent this, keep your palms open—if you don't have a grip, you can't pull.

a

b

▶ POSITION

Lie on your back on a bench, bend your knees and hips to 90 degrees, and position your feet so that your shins are parallel to the bench and your thighs are perpendicular to it. Anchor yourself to the bench by bending your elbows and using your hands to hold the pad above your head.

▶ TECHNIQUE

1. Brace your abdominals and lift your hips slightly off the bench. This is the starting position. Keep your hips off the bench for the duration of the set. Use your lower abdominals to move your hips up and in toward your ribs.

2. Continue moving through your full range of motion, stopping just before you lose tension in your abdominals.

3. Return to the starting position, but then move past it by stopping movement in your spine and lowering your legs to extend the hip joint. Lower your legs slowly and with control; this part of the movement is very demanding. Stop just before your abs lose the ability to hold you up. This shouldn't take too long! This extra countermovement greatly increases the demand on both the inner and outer abs. Lift your legs with fixed hips to begin the next rep.

▶ PERFORMANCE TIPS

Make sure that your hip joint is fixed as your hips move up. You are using your abdominals, especially the lower ones, to move your entire lower body without changing the position of your hips and knees. Move down by uncrunching your torso. Keep the position of your torso and hips fixed as you lower your legs to add an extra challenge. If you are moving fast, you are not using proper technique.

STARTING POSITION

HIPS LIFT UP AND IN TOWARD RIBS

LEGS LOWER TO EXTEND HIP JOINT

▶ **POSITION**

You will need either a bench or a flat abdominal board (the kind with bolsters for performing traditional sit-ups). Lie on your back on the bench or board, with your knees and hips bent and your feet placed flat on the bench or board. Anchor yourself by bending your elbows and holding the pad above your head (for the bench) or the handle or bolsters (for the board).

▶ **TECHNIQUE**

1. Brace your abdominals and lift your hips off the bench or board. Use your lower abs to move your hips up and in toward your ribs.

2. When your legs are positioned over your hips, straighten one knee and tuck the other one in (photo a). Hold this leg position while using your abs to lower your hips and legs as far as you can with control (photo b). As your back and hips return to the bench, maintain tension in your abs by keeping the full weight of your back and hips from sinking into the bench.

3. Return to the top of the movement, pause, switch legs, and repeat the movement.

▶ **PERFORMANCE TIPS**

This position of one leg in and one leg out may be familiar because it is just like the motion of a bicycle crunch. This exercise freezes the leg position and goes through a movement similar to the reverse crunch. Like the other exercises in this section, if you are moving rapidly, your technique is probably off, which presents less of a challenge for the abs. Each rep counts on this exercise! You don't do the reps per side on this one, since each rep will torch your abs. Sometimes less is more! Doing a lower number of quality reps will provide the best stimulus for your muscles, but getting through a high number of reps with any kind of movement will compromise your results.

a

b

▶ POSITION

Grasp the handles of a pull-up or chin-up bar and extend your legs to a position slightly in front of your hips. This starting position should make you feel your abs firing in a brace, creating tension in preparation for the exercise. Letting your feet hang freely and slightly out in front of you automatically creates tension for your abs.

▶ TECHNIQUE

1. Draw your legs toward your chest as high as possible, allowing your knees to bend.

2. Return your legs to the starting position, allowing your knees to straighten as you lower. Stop at the bottom of the movement and contract your abs hard to control any backward swinging of your body, and get ready for the next rep.

▶ PERFORMANCE TIPS

Choosing a starting position with your feet just slightly in front of your hips makes all the difference in the world on this exercise. Allowing your legs to flop down and behind you rests your abs between reps (and also makes you look silly). More importantly, this bad habit can set you up for injury by eliminating the tension in your inner abs. If your body starts swinging from front to back and you can't control it, you are likely moving too quickly. If you can't absorb and control the forces with your inner abs, they will transfer to your upper torso and arms (recall the whip analogy from chapter 1), and your body will begin to swing.

▶ VARIATION

You can perform a hanging bicycle knee raise by moving one knee up while your other leg remains in the bottom position. As you lower and straighten the raised knee, begin to raise and flex the knee of your bottom leg. This method may help prevent swinging. It also helps you develop strength in the proper ab muscles.

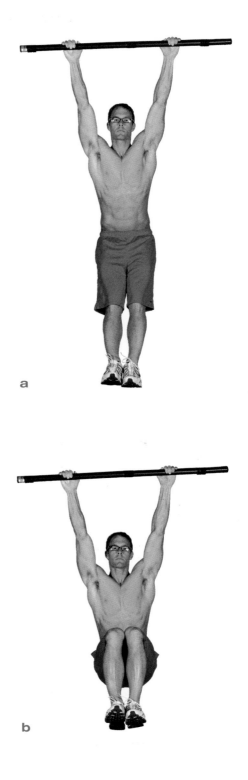

a

b

Hanging Leg Raise

a

b

▶ **POSITION**

Grasp the handles of a pull-up or chin-up bar and extend your legs to a position slightly in front of your hips. This starting position should help you feel your abs firing in a brace and tensing in preparation for the exercise.

▶ **TECHNIQUE**

1. Draw your legs up toward your chest as high as you can while keeping the legs straight.
2. Return your legs to the starting position. Stop at the bottom of the movement, contracting your abs hard to control any backward swing of your body, and get ready for the next rep.

▶ **PERFORMANCE TIPS**

Choosing a starting position with your feet just slightly in front of your hips makes all the difference in the world on this exercise. Allowing your legs to flop down and behind you rests your abs between reps (and also makes you look silly). More importantly, this bad habit can set you up for injury by eliminating tension in your inner abs. If you notice that your body starts swinging front to back and you can't control or stop it, you're probably moving too fast. If your inner abs can't absorb and control the forces, they will transfer to your upper torso and arms (recall the whip analogy in chapter 1), and your body will begin to swing.

▶ **VARIATION**

Perform a hanging bicycle scissor by stopping your legs when they are parallel to the floor. Next, move your legs away from each other in a scissor motion. Bring the legs back together in front of you and lower them to the starting position.

▶ POSITION

Find your loading point on the ball (see page 69). Place both hands behind your neck. As an alternative, place one hand behind your neck and the other one under your chin in a fist with your thumb down and your pinky touching your chin. This position helps you develop good habits of moving with your abs. It also keeps you from pulling on your head or dropping your chin for an unrealistic range of motion.

▶ TECHNIQUE

1. Use your abs to lift your chest up and forward in a crunching motion.
2. Stop when you feel the tension in your abs decrease.
3. Slowly return to the starting position.

▶ PERFORMANCE TIPS

Keep your torso a little bit open as you perform the crunch to prevent excessive spine flexion and to keep your inner abs engaged. Avoid bouncing off the ball at the bottom of the movement or taking your shoulders too far past your hips at the top of the movement. Both these habits will turn your abs off.

a

b

▶ POSITION

Find your loading point on the ball (see page 69). Place one hand behind your neck and the other one out to the side, holding your arm straight and your palm turned up toward the ceiling. This position increases activation of the inner abs and the obliques to keep you positioned on the ball, since your arm position creates a weight imbalance that your abs must counteract in order to keep you on the ball. Perform half of your reps with one arm out and half with the other arm out.

▶ TECHNIQUE

1. Use your abs to lift your chest up and forward in a crunching motion.
2. Stop when you feel the tension in your abs decrease.
3. Slowly return to the starting position.

▶ PERFORMANCE TIPS

Perform the crunch moving your torso as you would if you didn't have one arm out to the side. Keep your hips and shoulders squared—you should not rotate your torso at all. As you perform the crunch, keep your torso a little bit open to prevent excessive spine flexion and to keep your inner abs engaged.

a

b

▶ POSITION

Find your loading point on the ball (see page 69). Place your left arm across your chest with the elbow bent. Place your right arm straight out to the side with your palm facing forward. This position increases activation of the inner abs and the obliques since your arm position creates a weight imbalance that your abs must counteract to keep you on the ball. Each rep counts as one for this exercise (you are not doing reps per side).

▶ TECHNIQUE

1. Use your abs to lift your chest up and forward in a crunching motion.
2. As soon as you begin the crunch, start swinging both arms to the left. When you get to the top of the crunch, both your arms should be pointed directly overhead with the palms forward.
3. As you return, lower both arms to the left so that when you get to the bottom of the crunch, the left arm is straight out to the side with the palm forward and the right arm is across the chest to the left. As you perform the next crunch, repeat the arm movement in the opposite direction.

▶ PERFORMANCE TIPS

Move your torso to perform the crunch as you would if you didn't have your arms out to the side. Keep your hips and shoulders squared—there should be no rotation of the torso. As you perform the crunch, keep your torso a little bit open to prevent excessive flexing of the spine and to keep your inner abs engaged.

a

b

Crunch With Offset Torso on Stability Ball

▶ POSITION

Find your loading point on the ball (see page 69), but move your head and shoulders a bit further in toward the ball to slightly reduce the resistance from the loading point. (This is necessary because this exercise is more challenging, so you need slightly less resistance from your body weight resistance to start.) Place both hands behind your neck with the elbows bent and out to the sides. Take a couple of very small steps to the left so that your torso is positioned slightly to the left of the middle of the ball. (This position increases activation of the inner abs and the obliques since the asymmetrical body position creates a weight imbalance which your abs must counteract in order to keep you on the ball.) Perform half of your reps with your body offset to one side and perform the other half with your body offset to the other side.

▶ TECHNIQUE

1. Use your abs to lift your chest up and forward in a crunching motion.
2. Stop when you feel the tension in your abs decrease. Your shoulders should almost be over your hips.
3. Slowly return to the starting position.

▶ PERFORMANCE TIPS

You should still perform a straight crunch, moving your torso just as you would if you didn't have your body shifted slightly out to one side. Keep your hips and shoulders as square as possible. A small amount of rotation is unavoidable, since you have shifted your torso away from the middle of the ball, which is more balanced. As you perform the crunch, keep your torso a little bit open to prevent excessive spine flexion and to keep your inner abs engaged.

▶ VARIATION

For an even greater challenge, extend the arm on the same side as the shift. Essentially, you can combine the arm position from the offset-arm crunch with the offset body position of this exercise.

a   b

▶ POSITION

Find your loading point on the ball (see page 69). Place both of your arms overhead (almost parallel to the floor) with your palms facing up. Lift one foot a couple of inches off the floor and straighten the knee on that same leg. Perform half of your reps with one foot on the floor and half with the other foot on the floor.

▶ TECHNIQUE

1. Perform the crunch by driving the anchoring foot into the floor. At the same time, lift your torso up and forward, keeping your arms next to your ears. Your arms should remain mostly outside of your peripheral vision. They are simply hitching a ride on your torso providing an increased challenge to both your inner and outer abs.

2. Stop when your shoulders are almost on top of your hips.

3. Slowly return to the starting position.

▶ PERFORMANCE TIPS

The leg that is on the floor essentially helps you perform the crunch by driving your hips toward the ball as you use your abs to bring your torso over your hips. As you perform the crunch, keep your torso slightly open to prevent excessive spine flexion and to keep your inner abs engaged.

a   b

▶ POSITION

Begin by kneeling in front of the ball and placing your torso on it. Walking your body forward on your hands, roll out until your shins are on top of the ball. From a prone plank position with your shins on the ball and either your hands or forearms on the floor, shift your body to the left until your left leg is clear of the ball. Tuck it in toward your chest, keeping your right leg straight and positioned on the ball to support you. Perform all the reps on one side before switching and performing the exercise with your body off to the other side of the ball.

▶ TECHNIQUE

1. While maintaining a stable position that is supported by your abs, extend your left leg straight out into space. At the same time, flex your right leg and tuck it in toward your right elbow.
2. Continue cycling the free leg (left) while flexing and extending your right leg in opposition to your left, maintaining contact with the ball.

▶ PERFORMANCE TIPS

As with any plank, hold the position that puts your hips into a straight line with your shoulders and ankles. While performing the movement in this exercise, you will look like you are running in the air with one leg on the ball and one leg off the ball.

a

b

▶ POSITION

Get into a facedown plank position with your forearms and elbows folded on top of each other and resting on top of the ball. Brace your open hands against your biceps on each side. Place your feet wider apart than your hips to provide the necessary stability for this exercise.

▶ TECHNIQUE

1. Brace your abs and rotate your upper body to the left, going all the way around until the back of your upper right arm (triceps area) is on top of the ball.
2. Rotate back toward the starting position by pushing the right arm into the ball, keeping your abs braced hard.
3. Keep rotating to the right through the starting position to finish on the back of your upper left arm.

▶ PERFORMANCE TIPS

This is a very challenging exercise. The hardest part isn't starting the movement, it's stopping it! The biggest challenge lies in hitting the brakes at each end of the movement and reversing your direction to return to the middle of the ball. Control is essential, so do your best to manage your speed, which can easily accelerate rapidly, whipping you right off the ball.

a

b

Plank With Knee Tuck on Stability Ball

▶ **POSITION**

Get into a facedown plank position, resting your forearms and elbows on top of the ball. Place your feet either together or slightly apart.

▶ **TECHNIQUE**

1. Brace your abs and gently lift your right foot slightly off the floor (photo a). Tuck your right knee in toward your right elbow. With control, drive the knee in as far as you can (photo b).
2. Smoothly extend your knee backward and return your right foot to the floor.
3. Repeat this process with the left leg.

▶ **PERFORMANCE TIPS**

Emphasize controlled movement in this exercise. You will develop skill from managing the speed; control also develops strength. If you find yourself driving your knee in quickly and wobbling a lot on the ball, slow things down and give your body a chance to learn the movement. Using speed before you can control it prevents your brain from learning the technique.

a

b

▶ **POSITION**

Start facedown with your torso on top of the ball. Walking your body forward on your hands, roll out until you assume a push-up position. Your hands should be on the floor and your shins should be on top of the ball.

▶ **TECHNIQUE**

1. Brace your abs, bend from the hips, and drive your hips up toward the ceiling.

2. Your torso will stack over your head and hands while your legs roll up the ball. Your feet will be on the ball at the end of the movement.

3. As you lower your hips to return, drive your body backward and down past the starting position, keeping your elbows straight, so that your chest lowers toward the floor and the ball rolls up the front of your legs. In the final position, your body is fully extended in a straight line from your hands to your feet.

▶ **PERFORMANCE TIPS**

Although the top pike position looks more dramatic, the bottom position is actually more challenging. This is because the point of contact with the ground—your hands—is far away from your abs. The fact that you are accelerating into the end position from a pike makes stopping at the bottom even harder. Be sure you don't lower more than you can with control. It may be helpful to do the first couple of reps a bit more slowly until you find your safe range.

STARTING POSITION

PIKE POSITION

EXTENDED LAYOUT POSITION

▶ **POSITION**

Start facedown with your torso on top of the ball. Walking your body forward on your hands, roll out until your knees or your shins are on top of the ball.

▶ **TECHNIQUE**

1. Brace your abs, lift your left leg off the ball, and rotate your left hip up, allowing the left leg to rotate behind you so that the left foot moves toward the floor.

2. Stop at the end of your range of motion, then swing the left leg back around to the starting position on the ball next to the right leg. Both shins should be on top of the ball again.

3. While maintaining your ab bracing, perform the same motion with the right leg.

▶ **PERFORMANCE TIPS**

As with any exercise where you start in the center of the ball and rotate to an off-center position, it is harder to stop the movement than to start it. Control the movement with your abs so that once you start rotating, you can stop and return to the starting position smoothly. Beginning the movement with the other leg in the opposite direction is more demanding than you can imagine until you experience it!

a

b

▶ POSITION

Get into a push-up position with your toes suspended in the foot cradles. Begin with your feet directly under the anchor point.

▶ TECHNIQUE

1. Keeping your abs tight, drive your knees in toward your chest.
2. Drive your knees in as far as they will go—don't hold back! At the end of the movement, flex your hips and round your back slightly.
3. Return to the starting position by driving your legs backward while straightening your knees.

▶ PERFORMANCE TIPS

Lift your hips only as high as necessary to provide clearance for your knees. Moving your hips too high turns the exercise into a pike. For less resistance, walk your hands closer to the anchor point. For more resistance, walk your hands farther away from the anchor point.

a

b

▶ **POSITION**

Get into a push-up position with your toes suspended in the foot cradles. Begin with your feet directly under the anchor point.

▶ **TECHNIQUE**

1. Keeping your abs tight and your legs straight, lift your hips up toward the ceiling. Your torso will stack over your head and hands while your legs remain straight.

2. Return to the starting position with control by allowing the hips to lower.

▶ **PERFORMANCE TIPS**

Let your eyes and head point in the same direction as your chest. This means that at the top of the movement, you will be looking backward in the direction of your anchor point and feet, and the top of your head will be pointed toward the floor. Your brain gets a lot of input for how to control your spine from where your eyes are focused. Prevent looking at the floor during the movement, or you may end up there! For less resistance, walk your hands closer to the anchor point. For more resistance, walk your hands farther away from the anchor point.

a

b

▶ POSITION

Get into a push-up position with your toes suspended in the foot cradles. Begin with your feet directly under the anchor point. For less resistance, walk your hands closer to the anchor point. For more resistance, walk your hands farther away from the anchor point.

▶ TECHNIQUE

1. Keeping your abs tight and your right leg fixed straight in place, drive your left knee in toward your chest.

2. As your left knee begins to return to the starting position, immediately begin to tuck the right knee in toward your chest.

▶ PERFORMANCE TIPS

Moving too quickly will cause the TRX strap to saw back and forth and lose control. You will find it almost impossible to recover control without stopping and repositioning. Try to find the optimal combination of range of motion and speed to challenge your abs!

a

b

STARTING POSITION

CRUNCH POSITION

ELBOWS STRAIGHTEN FOR BODY SAW

▶ POSITION

Get into a prone plank position with your toes suspended in the foot cradles, your elbows bent, and your forearms on the floor. Begin with your feet directly under the anchor point. For less resistance, walk your elbows closer to the anchor point. For more resistance, walk your elbows farther away from the anchor point.

▶ TECHNIQUE

1. Keeping your abs tight, drive your knees in toward your chest as far as they will go.
2. At the end of the movement, your hips should flex slightly and your back should round slightly.
3. Return to the starting position by driving your legs backward while straightening your knees.
4. To create the sawing motion, move through the starting position and allow your elbows to straighten. Keep your abs as tight as possible. Use your inner abs to stop just before you lose control of your torso. It should be very easy to feel this point.

▶ PERFORMANCE TIPS

Be careful with this exercise; it is deceptively difficult! Your abs might even feel like someone is trying to saw you in half. As you move into the sawing motion, the difficulty will increase dramatically at the moment your shoulders pass over your elbows vertically. If you feel that your abs are about to give out, simply drop to the floor, reset the starting position, and begin again. It's important to know when to bail out on an exercise. In this case, if you're having a hard time maintaining control when moving with gravity, your abs will definitely fail on you when you stop and try to move against gravity.

▶ POSITION

Kneel under the TRX, placing your knees under the anchor point. Place your hands on the handles with open palms. For less resistance, walk your knees in front of the anchor point. For more resistance, walk your knees behind the anchor point.

▶ TECHNIQUE

1. Keeping your knees, hips, and shoulders in a straight line, allow your body to fall forward, controlling the movement and body position with your abs.

2. Your arms will sweep forward and up as you lower your torso and hips. At the end of the movement, your arms should be overhead and close to your ears.

3. Keep the abs tight to return yourself to the starting position with control, maintaining downward force on the handles.

▶ PERFORMANCE TIPS

If your hips are flexing, your body is forcibly shifting more of your body weight over your knees instead of letting it load into your torso and upper body. This is a reaction to excessive resistance. Your body simply won't let you go there without proper technique. The solution is to reduce the resistance by walking your knees forward until you find a position that allows you to perform the movement with proper technique.

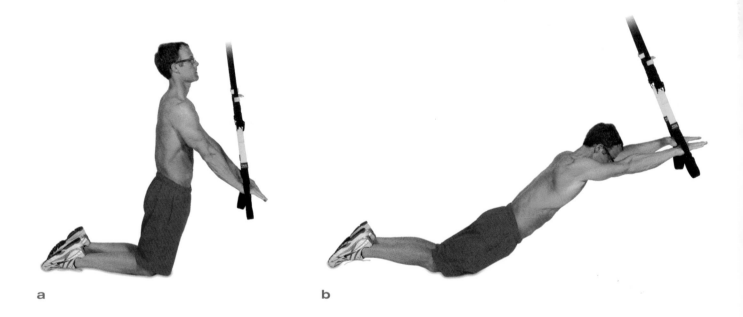

a   b

TRX Pull-Through

STARTING POSITION

CHEST MOVES TOWARD THIGHS

▶ POSITION

Lie on your back with your feet under the anchor point. Suspend your heels in the foot cradles. Sit up on your hips and place your hands flat on the floor just outside your hips in a position that is comfortable for your wrists. Keeping your arms straight, drive your hands into the floor to lift your buttocks. For less resistance, walk your hands closer to the anchor point. For more resistance, walk your hands farther away from the anchor point.

▶ TECHNIQUE

1. Use your abs to pull your hips inward, bringing your chest down toward the top of your thighs. Contract your abs hard to get the most out of this.

2. Now, drive your hips forward through the starting position and lift your hips up toward the ceiling, extending your entire body until your torso and legs are in a straight line facing the ceiling.

3. Swing down and back through the starting position to repeat the tucking motion of the hips. Be sure to fire those abs hard!

▶ PERFORMANCE TIPS

When you tuck your hips in, look at your thighs. When you lift your hips up, look at the ceiling. Your brain gets a lot of input for your spine from where your eyes are focusing. If you flex your neck forward to watch yourself doing this exercise in the mirror, you limit the range of motion during your hip lift. Try a couple of reps with your head incorrectly positioned and then a few with your head correctly positioned to feel the difference.

HIPS DRIVE FORWARD AND BODY EXTENDS

Carving a Cut Gut

It's time to take your exercises to the next level. By following the exercises in the previous chapters, your abs have become ready for just about anything. You will have a blast doing these exercises that blast your abs. These challenging but fun drills will accelerate the strength development of your abs. When performing these exercises, you'll be glad that you have trained your inner abs for antimovement, since you will be asking them to hold still while you challenge the outer abs in big ways. Simply performing these exercises will make you confident that you've got great abs even before you hit the beach. Those who do lots of crunches at the gym will be scared to even come near you.

These exercises make up the Scissors phase of your *Abs Revealed* workouts. This phase makes use of both old and new equipment. As before, some exercises use equipment (including the stability ball and TRX) and others do not. The new equipment in this phase includes the BOSU balance trainer and the slide. The BOSU balance trainer has become very prolific. Although Reebok introduced the slide decades ago, the concept didn't catch on until recently. The slide board (or more accessible versions like Valslides or gliding discs) is a terrific way to work your abs in a variety of angles while challenging stability and mobility. If you don't have access to slide equipment, you can use paper plates as a substitute.

In this phase, you'll perform difficult ab exercises that combine the main spinal directions of movement while maintaining strong stability (or antimovement) in the abs at the same time. Chapter 10 presents the programming for the exercises in the Scissors phase, which will get you cut!

Type of exercise	Page number
Floor and basic equipment	93
Stability ball	98
TRX	102
Slide and BOSU balance trainer	109

Make Things Harder

You can make the exercises in this book harder anytime you want. All you need to change is yourself. By changing your body position, you can add a resistance challenge, a stability challenge, or both. You can add resistance (load) to any exercise by changing the position of your torso, arms, or legs. Performing exercises asymmetrically really enhances the challenge. The uneven weight distribution makes your abs work harder at antimovement. Alternatively, decreasing the stability of any position also adds challenge. The cool thing is that there's nothing to learn; you've already been doing this! In chapter 5, you learned exercises that illustrate this concept at work, such as the offset-arm crunch on stability ball and the offset-torso crunch on stability ball. In the first one, you keep your torso in the same position and stick your arm out to the side. In the second one, you move your torso off to the side, but keep your arms in the standard crunch position. Both variations provide a new challenge.

▶ POSITION

Lie on your back with your left knee bent and drawn up toward your chest. Your right leg should be straight and lifted off the floor. Place your hands gently behind your neck or the lower part of your head. Your elbows should be bent and out to the side.

▶ TECHNIQUE

1. With your left knee bent and your right leg straight, lift your right shoulder off the floor (photo a) and move your right elbow toward your left knee. Move the elbow as close as you can to the knee.

2. As you return your right shoulder to the floor, begin to extend the left leg while simultaneously bending the right knee and bringing it in. When your right shoulder returns to the floor, your legs should be bent and positioned next to each other about halfway in.

3. As the right knee moves farther in, begin to lift your left shoulder off the floor and to move your left elbow toward your right knee (photo b).

▶ PERFORMANCE TIPS

The old-school, gym-class version of the bicycle crunch barely worked the abs at all. It usually consisted of lying on your back and kicking your legs furiously while pulling your head forward and rotating it vigorously from side to side. With your level of strength, you could likely do this version all day, but there's no point. The old version isn't even really a crunch because the hips and ribs do not move toward each other. Do the modern version presented here. Go slowly and lift your shoulder blades off the floor. When you bring your shoulders down, touch them to the floor but do not rest them there. This maintains constant tension in your abs. If you feel your ribs pop up as you touch your shoulders on the floor, you're resting too much weight on the floor.

a

b

Flying Bicycle Crunch With Medicine Ball

▶ **POSITION**

Sit on your hips on the floor with your left knee bent and tucked in and your right leg straight and raised off the floor. Your arms should be straight and out to the side. Hold a medicine ball in your right hand and lean back slightly, keeping your torso long and tall.

▶ **TECHNIQUE**

1. Begin to bend your right knee. As you bring it in, simultaneously bring your right and left arms together overhead.
2. Finish with both knees bent and positioned together and both arms straight overhead holding the medicine ball. Your torso will lift a little higher.
3. As you lower both arms to the side again, shift the ball to the left hand and begin to extend the left leg, leaning back just enough to maintain balance. Keep your torso long and straight.
4. Reverse the motion to return to the starting position.

▶ **PERFORMANCE TIPS**

This exercise is all about coordination. You will likely find it tricky for the first few reps, but you'll get it in no time. Once you do, you'll get into a nice rhythm, working your inner and outer abs hard to do the movement and to keep all of your body parts in the right place at the right time.

a   b

▶ POSITION

Grasp the neutral-grip handles of a pull-up or chin-up bar and draw your knees up toward your chest. Pull yourself up halfway so that your elbows are bent to approximately 90 degrees. Holding this starting position can be a big challenge!

▶ TECHNIQUE

1. Keeping your knees bent, rotate your hips as far to the left as your abs will allow. Do this with control, maintaining the position of your shoulder and torso with your arms and your abs.
2. Return your legs to the starting position.
3. Repeat the motion of the leg and hip on the right.

▶ PERFORMANCE TIPS

Your obliques will work very hard on this exercise. It does not require a lot of reps! Your abs must hold your body at an angle against gravity while simultaneously controlling the rotation of your legs. Be sure to rotate your hips slowly at first, since gravity will cause your legs to accelerate, putting your abs in a position that is increasingly challenging. Since you will have less leverage for pulling yourself up, you can easily lose control or quickly drop to one side. Move slower than you think is necessary at first to get a sense of which range of motion you can control.

a   b

Bar Chop

► **POSITION**

For this exercise, you need a padded, weighted bar or a short barbell that is relatively light (not an Olympic barbell). Stand holding the bar with a grip that is slightly wider than your shoulders. Use an overhand grip with your left hand and an underhand grip with your right hand. Raise the bar by bending your right arm so that the right end of the bar rests just above your shoulder and by extending your left arm so that the left end of the bar points away from you.

► **TECHNIQUE**

1. Rapidly draw in your left arm by bending the left elbow while extending the right elbow. Rotate your torso and drop rapidly into a shallow squat.
2. At the bottom of the movement, your left elbow will be bent, drawing the left end of the bar toward you. The right arm will be fully extended, holding the right end of the bar outside your left leg.
3. Rapidly rise out of the movement, using the rotation of the trunk to create the force, and reverse the motion to return to the starting position.
4. Perform all the reps for this side. Next, switch the weight to the other side and perform the reps for that side.

► **PERFORMANCE TIPS**

This dramatic exercise basically combines a crunching motion with the powerful action of the obliques to start and stop the rotation. Your arms steer the weight, but your abs are the engine that moves the bar. You will feel the involvement of your entire trunk. Your weight choice for the bar should range between 10 to 40 pounds (4.5 to 18 kg) with 40 pounds as an absolute maximum! The first time you try it, err on the lighter side and use the speed of your movement to create the challenge. The key to making this exercise work is to find the right mix between the weight of the bar and the speed of movement to load the abs for a proper challenge.

a   b

▶ POSITION

Stand in front of a pulley machine that is set up with two overhead handles. Grasp a handle in each hand. Lift the weight off the stack just enough to load your arms while keeping them overhead. Take a small step back (especially if you are tall) to ensure that you don't let the weight stack rest between reps. Stand with feet slightly wider apart than your hips.

▶ TECHNIQUE

1. Fire your abs to perform a crunch that is slightly angled to the left, keeping your arms fixed to transfer the weight from the cables to your abs.
2. Continue the motion, using your abs to bring your chest toward your left knee.
3. At the bottom of the movement, your right arm should reach down between your legs and your left arm should reach down outside your left leg.
4. Use your abs to control your return to the starting position.
5. Perform the next rep in a similar fashion, moving toward your right leg this time.

▶ PERFORMANCE TIPS

Avoid pulling with your arms. Think of your arms as steel rods without muscles that attach your abs to the cables. If you do the work with your abs, your arms will simply come along for the ride. Since the weight pulls you back up, be sure to pay extra attention to the return so that your abs work to slow the movement near the top. Prevent coming up so high that you lose the tension in your abs.

a   b

▶ POSITION

Lie on your back on the ball and find your loading point (see page 69). Place both fists under your chin as if you are boxing.

▶ TECHNIQUE

1. Shift your torso to the right, supporting most of your weight on your right leg, and extend your left leg as if you were kicking. At the same time, perform a crunch by moving your right shoulder toward your left leg.
2. As your left foot returns to the floor, shift your torso back to the center of the ball to the starting position.
3. Immediately repeat the movement by extending your right leg and crunching your left shoulder toward it as you shift to the left side of the ball.

▶ PERFORMANCE TIPS

You'll look a little bit like a kickboxer while performing this crunch. Kicking with one leg while performing a crunch makes you look like you are bobbing and weaving your upper body to duck a punch.

a   b

▶ POSITION

Lie on the ball facedown, fully bending your elbows and placing them on the ball with your forearms flat. Your legs should be extended, and your toes should be tucked under on the floor. Position your feet together or only slightly apart.

▶ TECHNIQUE

1. Brace your abs and gently lift your right foot slightly off the floor. Next, tuck your right knee in toward your left elbow.

2. Drive the knee in as far as you can with control. Your back will round slightly forward as you tuck your knee in.

3. Smoothly extend your knee backward and return your right foot to the floor.

4. Repeat this process with the left leg.

▶ PERFORMANCE TIPS

Emphasize controlled movement on this exercise. You will develop skill from managing the speed, which will also help you develop strength. If you find yourself driving the knee in too quickly and wobbling a lot on the ball, slow down and give your body a chance to learn the movement. Using speed too early before you can control it prevents your brain from learning the technique.

a

b

Rotating Crunch With Lateral Arm Swing on Stability Ball

▶ POSITION

Lie on your back on the ball and find your loading point (see page 69). Reach both arms to the right and rotate your torso to the right.

▶ TECHNIQUE

1. Use your abs to begin lifting your chest up and forward in a crunching motion.
2. As you continue into the crunch, rotate your arms and shoulders to the left. Your arms should be directly overhead at the top of the crunch—your shoulders will be almost over your hips.
3. As you lower your torso in preparation for the next rep, rotate your shoulders and arms to the left.

▶ PERFORMANCE TIPS

You should rotate while crunching. The extra weight of extending both arms to the same side you're rotating toward at the bottom of the crunch greatly increases the challenge of this exercise.

a

b

▶ POSITION

Start facedown with your torso on top of the ball. Walking your body forward on your hands, roll out until your shins are on top of the ball.

▶ TECHNIQUE

1. Brace your abs, lift your left leg off the ball and rotate your left hip up, allowing your left leg to rotate behind you to the right as your left foot moves toward the floor.

2. Stop at the end of your range of motion, and then swing your left leg back around toward the starting position.

3. Keeping the left leg off the ball, move past the starting position, bend your left knee, and pull it underneath you toward your right elbow.

4. Carefully extend your left leg through the hole created by your right arm, your torso, the ball, and the floor.

5. Pull your left leg back through the hole. Repeat the motion by performing both parts of the exercise with the left leg.

6. Perform all the reps with the left leg, take a short break, and then complete the reps with the right leg.

▶ PERFORMANCE TIPS

As with any exercise where you start on the center of the ball and rotate off center, the hardest part isn't starting the movement, it is stopping it. The greatest challenge lies in controlling the movement with your abs so that you can smoothly stop and start once you start rotating.

STARTING POSITION

LEG ROTATES BEHIND

LEG EXTENDS UNDER AND THREADS THE NEEDLE

Elevated Oblique Crunch With TRX

▶ **POSITION**

Get into a push-up position with your toes suspended in the foot cradles. Begin with your feet directly under the anchor point. Modify the push-up position by placing your right hand farther away from your feet. This will create extra space for driving your knees farther during performance of the exercise.

▶ **TECHNIQUE**

1. Keeping your abs tight, drive your knees in toward your right arm (photo a) as far as they will go—don't hold back!

2. At the end of the movement, your hips should flex and your back should round slightly.

3. Return to and through the starting position by driving your legs backward while straightening your knees. The momentum will carry your body past the starting position (photo b). Allow this to happen, but control the movement.

4. After your body swings slightly out to the left, repeat the original motion by tucking and pulling your knees toward your right arm.

5. Perform all your reps to the right side, take a short break, and then repeat on the left side.

▶ **PERFORMANCE TIPS**

The swinging out while in an extended position hits your abs extra hard because they need to hit the brakes in order to stop the motion. When tucking, lift your hips only as high as necessary to provide clearance for your knees. Moving your hips too high turns the exercise into a pike. For less resistance, walk your hands closer to the anchor point. For more resistance, walk your hands farther away from the anchor point.

a   b

▶ POSITION

Get into a push-up position with your toes suspended in the foot cradles. Begin with your feet directly under the anchor point.

▶ TECHNIQUE

1. Keeping your abs tight and your legs straight, simultaneously swing your legs to the right and lift your hips up toward the ceiling. Your torso will stack over your head and hands while your legs will remain straight.

2. Return with control by allowing the hips to fall toward the center of the starting position.

3. Keeping your body moving, repeat the motion, this time swinging your legs to the left.

▶ PERFORMANCE TIPS

This exercise is similar to the pendulum pike (chapter 5), but adds the twist of performing each pike to the right and left. Let your eyes and head point in the same direction as your chest. At the top of the movement, you should look behind you toward the anchor point. Your brain gets a lot of input for how to control your spine from where your eyes are focused. Prevent looking at the floor during the entire movement. For less resistance, walk your hands closer to the anchor point. For more resistance (not that you should need it), walk your hands farther away from the anchor point.

a

b

▶ POSITION

Get into a push-up position with your toes suspended in the foot cradles. Begin with your feet directly under the anchor point. For less resistance, walk your hands closer to the anchor point. For more resistance, walk your hands farther away from the anchor point.

▶ TECHNIQUE

1. Keeping your abs tight, swing your body to the right. Drive your right knee toward your chest while keeping your left leg straight.

2. Begin straightening your right knee, allowing your body to sway to the left, and immediately tuck your left knee in toward your chest.

3. Continue to perform the in-and-out motion of the knees, allowing your body to swing from left to right.

▶ PERFORMANCE TIPS

This exercise is similar to the elevated mountain climber (chapter 5), but adds a rapid swing to the right and left as you perform the leg movement. Move quickly, but not too quickly! Otherwise, the TRX strap could saw back and forth, causing you to lose control. It is almost impossible to recover control without stopping and repositioning. Try to find the optimal combination of range of motion and speed that challenges your abs the most! Don't worry about trying to coordinate the movement, just drive your knees in and out as your body swings right and left.

a

b

▶ POSITION

Get into a push-up position with your right foot suspended in one of the foot cradles and your left leg hovering next to your right leg. Your left and right thighs should be close to parallel. Position your body so that your right foot is slightly in front of the anchor point.

▶ TECHNIQUE

1. Brace your abs, lift your left leg, and rotate your left hip up, allowing the left leg to bend at the knee and rotate behind you as the left foot moves toward the floor.

2. Stop at the end of your range of motion, and then swing your left leg back around toward the starting position.

3. Bend the left knee and pull it underneath you toward your right elbow.

4. Carefully extend your left leg through the hole created by your right arm, your torso, and the floor.

5. Pull your left leg back through the hole and repeat the motion by performing both parts of the exercise with the left leg.

6. Perform all the reps with the left leg, take a short break and then complete the reps with the right leg (left foot in the foot cradle of the TRX).

▶ PERFORMANCE TIPS

This is a very challenging exercise that requires high levels of strength, flexibility, and stability. As always, this combination is the secret to having the best abs. To perform this exercise, you need to start from a position in which your feet are slightly in front of the anchor point. This should provide all the challenge you need. If you do need to make it harder, you can walk your hands farther away from the anchor point.

STARTING POSITON

LEG BENDS AND ROTATES BEHIND

LEG EXTENDS UNDER AND THREADS THE NEEDLE

TRX Side Plank With Reach-Through

PICK UP HIPS AND EXTEND ARM

ARM REACHES AND HIPS LOWER

HIPS LIFT AND ARM REACHES UNDER

▶ POSITION

Get into a side-plank position with your toes suspended in the foot cradles, your left forearm on the floor, and your left elbow positioned directly under your left shoulder. Your right leg should be slightly in front of your left leg and your right heel should be placed against your left toes. Begin with your feet directly under the anchor point.

▶ TECHNIQUE

1. Keeping your abs tight, pick your hips up off the floor until your body is straight. Point your right arm at the ceiling and keep it straight.

2. Simultaneously reach your right arm behind you and lower your hips so that they barely touch (but do not rest on) the floor.

3. Lift your hips toward the ceiling while swinging your right arm forward and down, bending it slightly. Allow your torso to rotate to the left as your right arm drops toward the floor.

4. As you continue lifting your hips, reach your right arm underneath your torso as far to the left as you can while maintaining control.

5. Reverse the motion by rotating your right arm and torso up and around as far as you can. Allow the hips to lower as before.

6. Perform all the reps on one side and then switch to the other side.

▶ PERFORMANCE TIPS

Learning to coordinate this movement is tricky at first. Just remember, *hips down, arm up* and *hips up, arm down*. Keep your feet from rotating away from the starting position while you rotate the rest of your body. Your upper body rotates a lot, but your hips rotate only a little. Your top leg is in front to help stack your hips and to keep them in proper alignment. When transitioning from one side to the other, turn your chest down toward the floor to keep from collapsing on your back in sheer exhaustion. Turning face down automatically puts your feet in the proper position on the other side. Switching sides to face up moves your legs out of the proper position. You'll have to reposition before starting the exercise.

▶ POSITION

Get into a side plank position with your toes suspended in the foot cradles, your left forearm on the floor, and your left elbow positioned directly under your left shoulder. Your left leg should be slightly in front of your right leg and your feet should be positioned slightly apart. Begin with your feet directly under the anchor point.

▶ TECHNIQUE

1. Keeping your abs tight, pick your hips up off the floor until your body is straight. Position your right arm parallel to the floor, with your upper right arm placed next to your right ear (photo a).

2. Tuck your right elbow toward your feet as you pull your left knee up toward your right elbow. Contract your abs hard to touch the right elbow and left knee together (photo b), if you can.

3. Return to the starting position by simultaneously returning your right arm and your left leg to their original spots.

4. Perform all the reps on one side and then switch to the other side.

▶ PERFORMANCE TIPS

Your top leg should be placed slightly behind your bottom leg, and your top leg should move very little. When returning to the starting position, be sure to fully open your torso and extend both your top arm and your bottom leg. When transitioning from one side to the other, turn over on your back to face up, which automatically puts your feet in the proper position on the other side. If you turn over to face down, your legs will be switched from the correct position, and you'll have to reposition before starting the exercise.

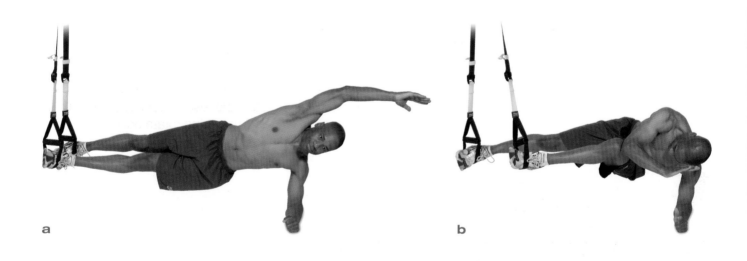

a   b

This exercise is the creation of Leigh Crews, TRX Master Trainer.

▶ POSITION

Lie on your back under the TRX with your head directly under the anchor point. Place your hands on the handles with open palms. Your arms should be straight and angled slightly out to the side.

▶ TECHNIQUE

1. Keeping your legs straight, lift them off the floor (photo a) while rotating both arms to the right as you perform a crunch (photo b).

2. As you return from the crunch, allow your arms to rotate back to the starting position and allow your legs to lower until they are hovering just above the ground.

3. Repeat the movement of the legs, this time reaching both arms to the left as you perform the crunch.

▶ PERFORMANCE TIPS

At the top of the movement, pull your hips up and contract your upper abs hard to lift your shoulder blades off the floor. When you lower your legs, your arms should be symmetrical and angled out slightly (in the start position). At the top of the V-up motion, you will have essentially performed a rotated crunch to one side.

a

b

▶ **POSITION**

Sit on the dome of the BOSU balance trainer, placing your tailbone approximately halfway between the base and the top. You may need to make small adjustments to your hip position once you start the exercise.

▶ **TECHNIQUE**

1. Lie back and extend your arms and legs so that your entire body is approximately parallel to the floor (photo a).

2. Brace your abs and quickly bend your elbows and knees to perform a crunch, tucking your knees in toward your elbows (photo b). At the end of the movement, you will momentarily form a ball on top of the BOSU.

3. Return to the starting position by extending the arms and legs simultaneously.

▶ **PERFORMANCE TIPS**

From the starting position, if you notice your body falling toward your hands or your feet, slightly adjust your hip position on top of the BOSU. If you are falling toward your feet, move your hips slightly higher. If you are falling toward your arms, move your hips slightly lower. Emphasize controlled movement in this exercise. Even if you begin in the correct set-up position, your hips may shift slightly after several reps to create an imbalance. If this happens, quickly reposition your hips and keep going!

a

b

▶ POSITION

Align your body in a position that is facedown and perpendicular to the slide board. Your feet should be on the board with your toes down, your knees should be bent, and your hands should be on the floor. If you are using a version of the slide that does not resemble a board, simply put your toes down on your sliding equipment and position your body as previously described. In the correct starting position, your knees will be bent at an angle that makes the shins approximately parallel to the floor.

▶ TECHNIQUE

1. Brace your abs and quickly drive your hips up slightly, rotating them to the left. You will finish with your left hip stacked on top of your right and the outside of your right foot on the slide.

2. Quickly reverse your motion to return toward the starting position. Continue through the starting position without stopping and repeat the motion to the other side, rotating your hips to the right. Finish with your right hip stacked on top of your left and the outside of your left foot on the slide.

▶ PERFORMANCE TIPS

The hardest part of this exercise is stopping the movement. After rotating right or left, it takes a massive effort to stop the motion of your body and return in the other direction. Pay attention to technique, since you will fatigue rapidly on this exercise. When your form fails, it's time to stop.

a

b

▶ POSITION

Align your body sideways along the length of the slide board. Your feet should be stacked on the board, with the outside of your right foot placed on the board. Your right elbow should be on the floor directly under your right shoulder and your hips should be off the ground. Your body should be aligned from head to toe.

▶ TECHNIQUE

1. Brace your abs and draw both knees in and up toward your torso while simultaneously lifting your hips a little higher to create more space for your knees to move. At the same time, rotate your torso very slightly.

2. Return your body to the starting position by sliding your right foot back where it came from and extending your knees. Perform all of your reps on one side and then switch sides.

▶ PERFORMANCE TIPS

You will hold a solid plank position throughout the exercise. The slight pike of the hips gives you a greater range of motion in your knees and lets you get a little rotation, thus adding to the challenge and the benefit for your abs. For even more challenge, try to switch sides without putting your hips down! After finishing your reps on the right side, turn your chest down toward the floor, lower your left elbow, and rotate your feet until the outside of your left foot is on the slide and you can lift your right elbow off the floor.

a

b

▶ POSITION

Align your body with the length of the slide board. Lie face down, almost parallel to the board, and assume a push-up position with your feet on the board and your toes down. Your hands will be on the floor very close to the end of the slide board. If you are using a nonboard version of the slide, simply put your toes down on your slide equipment and position your body as previously described.

▶ TECHNIQUE

1. Brace your abs and quickly drive your hips up into a pike while moving your feet toward your left hand. This will rotate your hips slightly to the left.

2. Return to the starting position and repeat the movement to the right. Alternate reps to each side until you have completed the set.

▶ PERFORMANCE TIPS

Your knees will need to bend slightly as you draw your feet in toward your hand. Be sure to return to the fully extended starting position. Don't cut corners by starting the next rep before your body is fully extended.

a

b

▶ POSITION

Align your body with the length of the slide board. Lie face down, almost parallel to the board, and assume a push-up position with your feet on the board and your toes down. Your hands will be on the floor very close to the end of the slide board. If you are using a nonboard version of the slide, simply put your toes down on your slide equipment and position your body as previously described.

▶ TECHNIQUE

1. Brace your abs and quickly drive your right knee in toward your chest as far as you can, allowing your right foot to slide along the board.

2. Rapidly return the right foot to the starting position while simultaneously drawing the left knee in and allowing the left foot to slide along the board. Continue alternating the motion on each side until you have completed the set.

▶ PERFORMANCE TIPS

Move quickly and keep your feet on the board at all times. This variation contrasts with traditional mountain climbers, in which your feet leave the ground as you jump and switch foot positions. For a more challenging variation, use your abs to hold one leg in a hovering position. Perform this variation with only one foot on the slide.

a

b

PART III

Programming and Planning

Setting Goals the Right Way

You must get your mind right in order to get your abs tight. You know that both your inner and outer abs need the right training to become strong, and you know that the right training and nutrition will change your body, helping your abs become visible. The workouts for these goals are presented in chapters 8 through 10. However, your mind might be the most powerful tool for getting the abs you want. This is because the way you approach your goals has a massive influence on your success.

To examine how this works, consider this book's explanation of your goals. It refers to "having the best abs possible," rather than "avoiding the worst abs possible." Your attitude about your training and nutrition must be unified and positive. This might sound overly simple, but it is powerful. Too many people get motivated to exercise by a negative experience, look, or feeling. This mentality of avoidance might give you the initial spark to get started, but in most cases, it doesn't sustain you to the achievement of your goals. Imagine listing the following as your fitness goals:

- Achieve the best-looking abs I've ever had.
- Be stronger in my abdominals than I've ever been.
- Have a well-balanced physique that makes me feel good, whether I'm on the beach or in the boardroom.

Let's get started! Those seem like motivating, positive goals. On the other hand, you might have more difficulty if you listed the following goals:

- Get rid of the flab on my abs.
- Stop feeling so weak.
- Stop feeling embarrassed to go to the beach.

These are essentially the same goals as the first list, but they set quite a negative tone. Don't focus on what you don't want to be. Instead, imagine what you want to do, who you want to become, and what you will achieve. If you're finding this motivational tool too touchy-feely, don't skip this chapter! Instead, think about a horror movie in which the soon-to-be victim is running away from the villain at full speed. He looks over his shoulder to make sure the bad guy isn't getting too close, then stumbles, trips, and gets caught. The victim was too focused on the negative thing behind him to see where he was going. Focus on where you are going, not on what you're escaping from.

When to Train Your Abs

If you ask enough people this question, you'll get equally passionate and well-reasoned responses that will be paradoxically both contradictory and logical. Should you do your ab exercises first, last, or in the middle of your other exercises? Does it even matter? You can approach the answer to this question in many ways. As with many questions in life, more than one right answer exists. Unfortunately, it's also one of those areas in which people just want a simple, straightforward, one-size-fits-all approach. This chapter lays it all out for you so you know how to proceed for your body, your goals, and your preferences.

By now, you know the importance of having strong and capable inner and outer abs. You also know that the inner abs have the primary task of preventing movement or creating stability to allow effective movement. These muscles are designed for endurance because they have to be stable all day long, both in and out of your workout routine. Thus, the textbook answer, based on the scientific and anatomical perspectives, is to train the abs last. If you fry your ab muscles and then hop under a bar for squats, you compromise your ability to use the abs to stabilize the trunk and protect the spine during this total-body lift.

What if you're one of those people who, when putting your ab exercises at the end of your workout, always skips them or puts in minimal effort? Maybe you run out of energy, run out of time, or simply hate training your abs. This just means that you don't like the burning feeling you experience in the abs when you train them hard. The science collides with the reality of your preferences, and your preferences usually win. You wind up skipping exercises, doing fewer reps, or

Can You Work Your Abs Every Day?

I have heard this question more times than I can count, and it's always asked by someone who is less than thrilled with the way his abs look. (No one has ever asked me if it's okay to train his hamstrings every day.) In this case, the answer to this question lies in another question that is far more important. If it were okay to work your abs every day, would you want to? You could wash your car every day, and you'd have a great-looking car. But the constant washing would get tiresome, tedious, and time-consuming.

Given that the abs play a critical role in movement, posture, and stability in daily activities, they are designed for endurance and for rapid recovery. This means you could train your abs every day. I've never recommended that anyone do so, and I'm not starting now. First, if you feel like training a muscle seven days a week, then you're not training that muscle hard enough even once a week. Hit it hard and then recover! Second, wouldn't you rather do something else with your time than put in unnecessary effort? This question shouldn't require much reflection. So, it's possible to work your abs every day, but there isn't really a good reason for doing so.

giving less than your best effort while performing the movements. This pattern isn't going to work if you want great abs. In this case, it may be best to break the rules. Yes, break the rules! This chapter sets out specific guidelines for exactly when and how to do this.

How do you break the rules the right way? The key to success with any exercise program is presenting your body with a stimulus that is progressively challenging. If you ask it to work harder than usual, your body will get better at doing what it is asked. Suppose you are fine with working your abs last; it's a good fit for you and you get great results doing it. At some point, your body adapts to the workout. You can change the exercises, but you can also provide a new challenge in many other ways. If you've been doing things in the correct order for a while, try moving your ab exercises to the beginning of your workout to make your abs work little harder during the other exercises. This is another example of when it's okay to break the rules. However, don't get the impression that the rules are pointless. The reality is that human physiology is complex, so you may need a bit of wiggle room. Still, you must have a purpose and a reason for doing these workouts. Here's a quick review of the guidelines that can help you decide when to break the rules:

- Do not break the rules when beginning a new workout or when using a lot of new, challenging exercises. Make sure you can switch on both the inner and outer abs at the right intensity and at the right time, coordinating them with the rest of your body.

- Do break the rules if your abs are a big priority for you (if you're reading this book, they probably are), but you find yourself performing your ab exercises halfheartedly at the end. Under these circumstances, it makes sense to put your best effort into what matters most. Use the energy you have earlier in your workout to put top effort into your ab exercises.

- Do break the rules if you've been doing the same workout for a few weeks and you need a new challenge, but you aren't quite ready to change the exercises. Perform your ab exercises early in your training session to make your ab muscles more tired for the rest of the routine.

Why is it okay to break the rules? It's all about your goals. You're reading this because you want to use a modern, intelligent approach to training and nutrition that doesn't suck all the joy out of living. You're not training to become a champion power lifter or a massively developed bodybuilder, or to achieve the highest vertical jump in your neighborhood. You just want to have as little body fat and as much muscle as you need to look fit, showing the abs as your centerpiece. For your goals, you're not training for maximum strength or power. Therefore, you can deal with fatigued abs when doing the exercises for the rest of your body.

Balancing Your Workouts and Your Life

If you put something on your calendar at a specific day and time, you somehow always get it done. Whether it's a dentist appointment, a job interview, or any other event that matters to you, you put it on your calendar. Too many people start the day with a vague notion that they need to work out at some point during the day. The workout gets knocked around by other priorities, and before they know it, it gets knocked off that day's to-do list. Give your workouts a fixed day and time. Make them compatible with your schedule. You can do this in many ways, whether you put it on your calendar the night before, plan out an entire week ahead of time, or set up a stable schedule that simply repeats every week. If a real emergency should arise, and these are few in life, you can simply move the workout to a different time on the same day or to a planned day off. Workouts should not simply disappear from your schedule.

Another pitfall people encounter is preserving their workouts when others make requests for their time. Many people worry that they are being selfish, or that others will find them selfish. The following scenarios can help you manage the demands on your time:

SITUATION 1. When someone asks for a favor of you that isn't life or death, say, "Sorry, but I have an appointment (or other commitment—choose one) at that time."

WHY IT WORKS. You don't owe someone an explanation every time you don't want to do something. We seem to have a societal problem with saying a simple no. We feel the need to explain why we have to decline, but we don't really have to explain. In this scenario, if you say, "I can't. I have to work out at that time," some people may think your reason seems selfish. To protect your reputation and your fitness goals, you can simply tell them you have another commitment.

SITUATION 2. Your supervisor gives you a project that should have been done yesterday, and you already have five projects like it. If you take on this extra work, you'll have to stay later, work harder, eat junk, and miss your workout. As your workout supervisor, I'm here to tell you that this behavior is not acceptable. You should say, "Okay, I'll get right on that. However, you'll need to tell me which one of these other projects can be put to the side so I can prioritize this one."

WHY IT WORKS. You demonstrate that you can and will make the new project your first priority, but you won't do so at the expense of all of your other commitments (both professional and personal). It's called having boundaries and it's the only way to succeed in fitness, in business, and in life.

Fitting in Fitness

How do you get results while living the rest of your life? Lots of trainers get this one wrong, but with good reason. Maybe they love exercise too much, since they chose to make a career of fitness. Whenever trainers hear clients state their goals, they immediately begin thinking of all the great programming ideas and exercises that will achieve those goals. Clients commonly ask the same question when they see their program for the first time, and it isn't "Will this help me reach my goals?" More often than not, it is "How long will this take?" Most trainers don't know how to answer because they didn't consider the question: The workout takes as long as it takes. This response is more common from newer trainers who are enthusiastic and know they can get results. Again, it comes from a good place, but fitness professionals are exercise fanatics. You want to get results while making time for all the rest of the stuff in your life.

Certainly, if you are reading this, your commitment level is high. This section literally makes your approach to exercise immune to excuses by making your workout fit any amount of time you have and by providing a strategy for those days when you're pressed for time. After all, no one lives in a perfect world.

Fitness in Real Time

The top reason people give for skipping exercise is a lack of time. Although this point is seriously debatable, let's skip it. It's more helpful to look at another aspect of the time problem. When people who currently exercise aren't getting the results they want, they often say they need to do more, and they usually mean more time! If you are one of these people, should you devote more time to working out when your time is already limited? Why try to use more of something you already have so little of? Instead, consider working harder with the time you have. If you're already spending 60 minutes exercising, adding 15 minutes at the same intensity probably won't provide the stimulus your body needs. A better option is to increase your intensity during that 60-minute workout.

Suppose you can do 20 minutes at 6 miles (10 km) per hour on a treadmill. Which of the following two options will help you get more fit?

- 25 minutes at the same speed
- 20 minutes with a speed increase of 1 mile (1.6 km) per hour

Five more minutes at the same speed that your body is used to would certainly burn more calories, but it won't give you a shock. It won't make your body sit up and take notice, and you gave up five more minutes of your time. Adding intensity to the existing time allotment will both burn more calories and move your body out of its comfort zone.

Finding the Right Intensity Level

For an exercise to provide the right stimulus for change, it should be comfortably uncomfortable. You should know that you are working, but you shouldn't feel like you're about to puke. Uneducated exercisers take their bodies to the point of nausea or vomiting. People who don't know how to the find the right intensity go over the edge to make sure that they've worked hard enough. It's as if, when filling a bathtub with water, the only way you knew that the tub was full was when the entire house flooded. Working too hard is just as misguided as not working hard enough.

Start figuring out how much time you have for exercise (even if you're already exercising) by answering the following questions honestly. Don't use a best-case scenario, since the planets don't align that often. Provide realistic, honest answers.

1. How many days per week can you commit to your exercise program?

2. How much time do you have available for these training sessions? It doesn't have to be the same amount every day.

3. Are some days simply too packed with other things? These should be scheduled as a rest day.

Right or wrong answers don't exist, only honest ones. Results aren't achieved by how much time you punch on the exercise clock, but by how much you challenge yourself during your exercise time. Apart from extreme answers to this question, almost any amount of time can work. Your results are all about intensity. However, if you have only 10 minutes a day, three days per week, you may need to give something up in order to devote more time to exercise. On the other hand, if you have two hours per day, seven days a week, you'll have more free time than you thought. The chapters that follow provide specific details on how to use these workouts on days that are both ideal and crunched for time. You'll create a system for doing a successful workout even when you don't have the ideal amount of time.

Continually ask yourself why. You want great abs. Why? You want to look good. Why? Keep asking why to form a connection to your goals that is deeper and more meaningful. The answer will give you a reason for every exercise you do and will help you overcome just about any obstacle to permanent fitness. This book gives you the *how*, but the *why* is all up to you.

Stage 1: Constructing the Core

It's time to begin your workouts, starting with the core. This is the first part of our Rock, Paper, Scissors theme. A sculptor seeking to create a beautiful work of art begins with a rock and chisels it into a thing of aesthetic beauty. Your abs are the rock, these workouts are your chisel, and you are the sculptor.

This chapter includes the specifics of workouts in the Rock phase and ties together the cardio plan laid out in chapter 2, the nutrition strategies identified in chapter 3, and the ab exercises presented in chapter 4 with complete week-by-week programs. It also provides specifics from chapter 7 on achieving effective workouts in the midst of life's ups and downs. Finally, it presents top tips for getting the most out of your workouts. Chapter 9 covers the Paper phase and chapter 10 lays out the Scissors phase.

Structure of the Workouts

Here's how each week of your workout looks. You'll get a start-to-finish plan for each training day, including warm-ups, resistance training, cardio training, and, of course, ab exercises. On some days, you will perform resistance training plus cardio, while on others, you'll perform cardio alone. All workout days will include some ab exercises.

Warm-Up

To get you ready for your workouts, we're going old school—sort of. A warm-up prepares your body for activity by doing the following:

- Increasing blood flow to the extremities
- Raising the temperature of your tissue
- Switching on your nervous system

In general, static stretching is best used after a warm-up. Think of your connective tissue and muscles as taffy. When taffy is cool, it is brittle, hard to stretch, and prone to breaking. When taffy is warm, it is soft, pliable, and easy to stretch. Your warm-up consists of two total-body exercises of your choosing that achieve the three preceding objectives. You can do jumping jacks, mountain climbers, explosive push-ups, squat jumps, walking lunges, pull-ups, kettle bell swings, medicine ball chops, and so on. You get the idea. Doing one set of each for 10 to 20 reps provides an ample warm-up. Be sure to choose one exercise that focuses primarily on the upper body and one that focuses on the lower body. For example, do squat jumps and pull-ups. If you have any overly tight muscles after your warm-up exercises, perform the appropriate static stretches to inhibit those muscles and give you a more balanced workout. Otherwise, include some static stretches after your workout.

Resistance Training

A total-body approach to resistance training is just as important to great abs as the ab exercises themselves are. By using the largest muscles in your body, you'll burn the most calories during the workout and get a higher post-workout response from your metabolism. This section lays out the basic format for your resistance-training workouts and shows you how to integrate your ab training. This format applies to the workouts in chapters 8 through 10. Your resistance-training routines will feature two different workouts (workout A and workout B). Simply alternate between the two each time you do resistance training.

In this chapter, the key difference between workout A and workout B is how you load your body for the exercises. Bilateral exercises (used in workout A) use both sides of your body symmetrically. Examples include squats, deadlifts, bench presses, and pull-ups. Unilateral exercises (used in workout B) use the sides of your body asymmetrically. Examples include single-leg squats or lunges, single-leg deadlifts, single-arm chest presses with a dumbbell, and single-arm pull-downs with a cable. Using bilateral and unilateral exercises gives you the best results, the best body, and the best abs, all while keeping your workouts from getting boring. Unilateral exercises force your abs to work hard to stabilize your body, while allowing your arms and legs to move with unbalanced weight. Bilateral exercises require your abs to provide stability for heavier, balanced weight. The bilateral exercises in this book are similar to exercises you already know and may have performed before. The unilateral exercises (used in workout B) are novel, challenging versions of the same exercises. Table 8.1 presents bilateral exercises and their unilateral counterparts.

Table 8.2 presents the six types of movements that will make up your resistance training. These six exercises provide a balanced, full-body workout, while the variations used in the A and B workouts cover all of the options for the move-

TABLE 8.1

Bilateral and Unilateral Exercises

Bilateral	Unilateral
Squat	Single-leg squat, lunge
Deadlift	Single-stiff-leg deadlift, suitcase deadlift (a regular deadlift with weight in one arm only)
Bench press	Single-arm chest press with dumbbell (or alternating dumbbell chest press)
Barbell row	Single-arm dumbbell row
Shoulder press	Single-arm shoulder press (or alternating shoulder press with dumbbell)
Pull-up or wide-grip lateral pull-down	Single-arm pull-down with cable

TABLE 8.2

Types of Movement in Resistance Training

Movement type	Example
Upper body: Horizontal pull	Row
Upper body: Horizontal push	Bench press
Upper body: Vertical pull	Pull-up
Upper body: Vertical push	Shoulder press
Quad-dominant lower-body exercise	Squat
Hip-dominant lower-body exercise	Deadlift

ments that humans perform (pushing, pulling, rotating, and standing on one or two legs). This way, your body will look great and will be ready for just about anything! Although you will find suggested exercises for resistance training in the sample workouts at the end of this chapter, you don't have to follow them precisely. All you have to do is color by number. Just fill in appropriate exercises for the movement types, and you're on your way!

Ab Exercises

As you know from discovering the link between the inner and outer abs, your body is a connected system. In truth, every exercise you do uses your abs to either stabilize (prevent unwanted movement) or mobilize (create movement) your body; only a few of the exercises exclusively require stability (that is, they require no movement at all). Most of the ab exercises in this book blend both stability and mobility, but they tend to feature one or the other to a greater degree. By now, you know that any movement requires stability to make it go; stable inner abs mobilize the outer abs.

Now that you are getting down to the workouts, try differentiating the ab exercises from part II according to the characteristic the exercise emphasizes most—stability or mobility. This process makes it much easier for you to choose exercises for the workouts. You will choose a specified number of stability and mobility exercises for each workout. Chapters 8 through 10 include tables that categorize the abdominal exercises according to whether they primarily require

Weight Belts: Don't Wear a Girdle, Build One!

If you're following the training programs in this book, you should know better than to wear a weight belt! The transversus abdominis muscle already provides natural support. If you train your abs right, you should never need a weight belt. Those poor souls who lumber through gyms for hours on end doing every single exercise with a weight belt are building weaker abs. Cinching a weight belt tightly against your midsection places a lot of force on your ab muscles. Your abs respond by forcefully pushing back out.

Remember, bracing is your technique for weight training. Your abs are drawn neither in nor out. Training while pushing the abs out weakens them. If you only feel strong when using props, belts, and wraps to keep your joints in place, you aren't really getting stronger. You are only as strong as the weakest part of your body. Human beings have done heavy lifting for millennia without weight belts. Belts are only appropriate if you are power lifting competitively or going for a low-rep maximum lift. There's no need to buy a girdle if you're training your abs the right way.

stability or mobility. Differentiating the exercises in this manner helps you fill in the blanks when you are ready to break the rules (see chapter 7 for more information) by reversing the order of your workouts.

Cardio

Your cardio consists of either zone training (ZT) or high-intensity interval training (HIIT). You can use one approach exclusively or you can use both. Since they both work, they are included here to provide options that fit your training style, preferences, energy levels, and time from day to day. There's more than one way to skin the fat!

If you haven't already done the test for VT1 HR (ventilatory threshold 1 heart rate) from chapter 2 (refer to page 15), now is the time to do it. Remember, if you plan to always perform your cardio workouts separately from your resistance-training workouts, even on days when you do resistance training plus cardio, you should only perform the test once. You should also perform it separately from any other form of exercise. If you plan to perform your cardio immediately after your resistance-training workouts (concurrent training), you need to perform the test twice on separate days. One test should be completed right after resistance training, and the other test will be a separate effort. The reason for this is that the testing conditions must match the performance conditions. Simply follow the instructions for the test (see page 16), record your VT1 HR measurements, and note your results for zones 1 and 2. Be certain to label the results so you know which ones are from the concurrent-training test and which ones are from the other test. Use the correct numbers for the corresponding type of training day.

The workouts provide instructions for the total cardio time of both options. In ZT cardio, you'll spend this time alternating between zones 1 and 2. The total time and length of intervals is also provided for HIIT cardio. Neither option includes times for warm-up or cool-down, so be sure to allow a few minutes at the beginning and end for each.

If you're using HIIT cardio, keep these two important points in mind: The definition of *high intensity* is very personal. It is different for each person. The speed, resistance level, and incline you need for a high-intensity experience might be different for someone else. You should also understand that this threshold will change as you get more fit, so you may need to increase the challenge by changing speed, resistance level, and incline over time. The HIIT workouts become progressively more challenging in terms of total time and interval lengths, but you may also need to change these factors.

Guidelines for Success

The following guidelines are the glue that holds your workouts together. It's one thing to know the purpose of the exercises and the details of sets and reps, but these are just numbers and words on a page. When you actually start doing a workout in the real world, you need some helpful tips to make sure you are getting the most out of your effort and time.

Use Your Workout Time Effectively

For most readers, the best approach will be to use supersets for workout A. You simply pair up two exercises and perform set 1 of the first exercise, followed by set 1 of the second exercise. Repeat this pattern until you have done all four sets for each exercise. If you have more time to devote to your exercise plan than most people do, you can perform the exercises as straight sets (doing all sets of each exercise together), resting between sets. After laying out the full workouts, this chapter shows you how to handle those days when you don't have as much time as you had hoped for!

Train for the Feeling, Not the Number

With all your workouts and exercises, both resistance and cardio, the key to progress is finding a challenge that is big enough to make your body change but small enough to avoid overtraining. Use these guidelines to guarantee progressive resistance-training workouts. Your goal is 10 reps in workout A, 20 reps in workout B, and a variation for your ab exercises. As you do your workouts, always try to do more than the number of reps set out in the goal. If you can do at least two more reps than the goal number, you should increase the challenge. This can be done in a number of ways. You can increase the resistance, do more sets, take less time for rest, or work out more days per week, to name a few. Since you won't be standing around much between sets as it is, the best choice for keeping your workout time relatively constant is to increase the resistance.

You will see ranges of reps that are somewhat larger for the ab exercises, since you'll be getting resistance from your body weight. Also, each exercise provides a different challenge for each reader. Remember to train for the feeling, not the number. If you see a rep range of 6 to 12 for a given exercise, you should not always be doing either six reps or 12 reps. You want your muscles to fatigue somewhere between the two figures. Sometimes you'll do seven reps, and other times you'll do 11. If you're always stopping at the higher number in the range, you need a new challenge. Your muscles don't count reps and they don't know that they are supposed to be tired when the counter hits the upper limit of the range.

Don't worry about progressing through the cardio. The routines become progressively harder by either adding time to the duration of the total workout or lengthening the efforts of the intervals. People who simply stay on the machine until their time is up are training for the number. However, you'll still be training for the feeling, since both ZT and HIIT cardio take your body outside of its comfort zone.

Use a Training Journal

Using a training journal to record your workouts prevents you from simply repeating the same workout over and over again. How long does it take you to remember what you had for dinner three nights ago, if you can remember at all? Can you recall your workouts any better? How much weight did you use for each exercise and how many reps did you do? Even if you could remember these details, you probably wouldn't be able to recall whether the workout was hard enough. You'd likely repeat the same weight for the same amount of reps each workout, maintaining the same body. The number one reason why people fail to get results from their workouts is that their routines are not progressive.

I've been journaling since before I became a trainer, and it has always made sense to me. We track our investments, stats for fantasy sports teams, bank deposits, and anything else that really matters to us. If the results of your workouts are important to you, tracking what happens during a workout so you can make smart choices for the next one should be a no-brainer. The point is to help you dial in the right resistance to maximize the benefit of your exercise efforts and time.

You'll need to get a training journal or any other type of notebook you find convenient. Before the workout, make a list of your exercises. During the workout, record what you do and make notes to yourself to help with future workouts. If a weight was too light, draw an up arrow next to it. If it was too heavy, write a down arrow. The next time you do that workout, you'll have an easier time challenging yourself. You can also create and use any other shorthand notations that work for you. During cardio, you can write down the details of the speed or resistance you used on the cardio machine, the total amount of time you spent, or the number of intervals you did. Journaling about cardio workouts is not as essential as recording resistance training, but do it if you know it will help you stay on track. This will prevent you from failing to get results from your workouts. Using a training journal is the best way to make sure you are progressing in your workouts. Knowing what you did last time helps you adjust the intensity for next time.

Use Different Lifting Speeds

Another terrific source of challenge and variety for your workouts is to change the lifting speed. When your weights are heavier and unbalanced, as in workout A, you will use more traditional speeds and lift them with control. When your weights are lighter and unbalanced, as in workout B, you will lift them faster, which increases the demand on your abs, making the muscles work harder and giving you better results. The exercises in workout B also introduce a stability challenge. This is one more way to make the workouts feel distinct, different, and interesting.

In Case of Emergency: Smash the Clock

What if you don't have time for a full workout? This chapter promises an easy-to-follow recipe for those days when the universe has its way with your schedule. Too often, when other demands encroach on workout time, people skip the workout because they don't have time to do it. In reality, you may not have time for the full workout, but you can still work hard enough to give your body a challenge. An effective workout isn't determined by how much time passes while you do it—just ask the poor souls who pedal lightly on the stationary cycles at the gym for an hour at a time and never see any results—it's determined by what you do with the time you have.

If time is short, use Ross' rule of thirds. Use one-third of your time on resistance training, ab training, and cardio training. That's it. Divide up the time you have into three equal segments and perform each of the main parts of your workout for that length of time. When the time is up, stop and move on to the next thing. For example, suppose you have 30 minutes to exercise. You would perform 10 minutes of weight training, perhaps doing one set of each of your exercises and maybe another set of some of them. Once 10 minutes is up, move on to your ab exercises. Finally, do 10 minutes of cardio. Since your time is so short, if you're doing ZT cardio, modify your intervals to shoot a little higher than zone 2 for your heart rate. That way, you get just as tired in 10 minutes as you would during a full workout. You would probably only need 10 minutes for HIIT cardio, anyway. On those days when you're pressed for time, use Ross' rule of thirds to put your best effort into the time you have!

Placement of Ab Exercises

The Rock phase follows the rules of ab exercise placement by putting them at the end of your workouts. There is one exception to this rule. In this phase, do the first four exercises from chapter 4 (the supine draw-in, supine brace, prone plank, and side plank) as the first activity in each workout. These foundational four are the only exercises in this text that focus exclusively on stability, asking you to simply hold a position of your body against gravity. They are meant to set the stage for better movement by giving your inner abs a wake-up call and helping you unconsciously use these muscles. Table 8.3 provides instruction on performing this sequence of exercises.

TABLE 8.3

Foundational Four

Exercise	Sets	Reps	Exercise page number
Supine draw-in	2	Hold for 10 sec.	44
Supine brace	4	Hold for 10 sec.	45
Prone plank	1	Hold for 30 sec.	46
Side plank	1	Hold for 30 sec. per side	47

Nutrition

Don't forget nutrition, which is the real key to results. Remember, you'll begin working your list of prioritized nutrition changes during the Rock phase. Specifically, work on the top two items on your list for the greatest impact on your results. Spending three weeks to make them part of your new routine allows you to take a big step forward, and sets the stage for the next items on your list for the next part of your training, the Paper phase.

Schedule for Rock Phase

This section presents your weekly training schedule. At the beginning of the schedules for weeks 2 and 3, you'll find a summary of changes for that week so you can move through them without any surprises. Next, you will find sample workouts to show you what the schedules look like in practice. Be sure to check out www.AbsRevealed.com for additional information on workouts and exercises.

WEEK 1

Resistance Training Plus Cardio: Three Days Per Week (Alternating Workouts A and B)

WORKOUT A: DAYS 1 AND 3

Foundational four

Warm-up: Choose two body-weight exercises.

Resistance training: Choose six bilateral exercises.

Ab exercises: Choose four exercises from the following table. Complete two sets of each as a circuit (perform all four exercises once, rest 60 seconds, and perform all four again).

Cardio: Complete 15 minutes of ZT or complete 8 minutes of HIIT.

Exercise name	Reps	Exercise page number
Reverse crunch with hand targets	15	48
Dead bug	8-10 per side	49
HTIL crunch	10	50
Negative crunch with control	10	51
Quadruped draw-in with arm and leg movement (bird dog)	5-6 per side	52

WORKOUT B: DAY 2

Foundational four

Warm-up: Choose two body-weight exercises.

Resistance training: Choose six unilateral exercises.

Ab exercises: Choose four exercises from the table and complete two sets of each as a circuit.

Cardio: Complete 15 minutes of ZT or complete 8 minutes of HIIT.

Cardio Only: Two or Three Days Per Week

Foundational four

Ab exercises: Choose four exercises from the table and complete two sets of each as a circuit.

Cardio: Complete 21 minutes of ZT or complete 12 minutes of HIIT.

Cardio Schedule for Week 1

ZT Cardio

Type of training day	MINUTES						
	3	6	9	12	15	18	21
Resistance training plus cardio	Zone 1	Zone 2	Zone 1	Zone 2	Zone 1		
Cardio only	Zone 1	Zone 2	Zone 1	Zone 2	Zone 1	Zone 2	Zone 1

HIIT Cardio

Type of training day	Total time	Interval instructions
Resistance training plus cardio	8 min.	Alternate between 30 sec. of very intense exercise (such as sprinting) and 30 sec. of lower-intensity activity (such as walking or full rest).
Cardio only	12 min.	Alternate between 30 sec. of very intense exercise (such as sprinting) and 30 sec. of lower-intensity activity (such as walking or full rest).

What's Different This Week?

Resistance training is now four days per week. ZT cardio is now 21 minutes on resistance-training days and 27 minutes on cardio-only days. In HIIT cardio, the rest interval decreases by 10 seconds. You'll expand your abdominal exercises in both number and variety, choosing different exercises for days of resistance training or cardio. For both types of training days, choose any of the exercises from chapter 4 (except the foundational four). You can choose exercises based on your preferences and available equipment. The table that follows will help you determine whether the exercises focus primarily on mobility or stability.

Exercise name	Primarily stability or mobility	Reps	Exercise page number
Reverse crunch with hand targets	Mobility	15	48
Dead bug	Stability	8-10 per side	49
HTIL crunch	Mobility	10	50
Negative crunch with control	Mobility	10	51
Quadruped draw-in with arm and leg movement	Stability	5-6 per side	52
STABILITY-BALL EXERCISES			
Roll-up	Mobility	6-12	53
Side plank	Stability	Hold for 30 sec. per side	54
Reverse crunch	Mobility	6-12	55
Semi-vise crunch	Mobility	6-12 per side	56
Vise crunch	Mobility	6-12	57
Vise crunch with leg roll	Mobility	5-10	58
Leg drop with ball balance	Stability	6-10	59
Plank with elbows on ball	Stability	Hold for 30 sec.	60
Plank with shins on ball	Stability	Hold for 30 sec.	61
TRX EXERCISES			
Leg raise	Stability	6-10	62
Resisted roll-up	Mobility	8-15	63
Assisted roll-up	Mobility	8-15	64
V-up	Mobility	8-15	65

Only choose from the first five exercises if they are still challenging you at the end of week 1 or 2.

Resistance Training Plus Cardio: Four Days Per Week (Alternating Workouts A and B)

WORKOUT A: DAYS 1 AND 3

Foundational four

Warm-up: Choose two body-weight exercises.

Resistance training: Choose six bilateral exercises.

Ab exercises: Choose five exercises (three for mobility and two for stability). Complete two sets of each as a circuit (perform all five exercises once, rest 60 seconds, and perform all five again).

Cardio: Complete 21 minutes of ZT or complete 8 minutes of HIIT.

WORKOUT B: DAYS 2 AND 4

Foundational four

Warm-up: Choose two body-weight exercises.

Resistance training: Choose six unilateral exercises.

Ab exercises: Choose five exercises (three for mobility and two for stability). Complete two sets of each as a circuit (perform all five exercises once, rest 60 seconds, and perform all five again).

Cardio: Complete 21 minutes of ZT or complete 8 minutes of HIIT.

Cardio Only: One or Two Days Per Week

Foundational four

Ab exercises: Choose five exercises (three for mobility and two for stability); choose different exercises than those you used for days of resistance training plus cardio. Complete two sets of each as a circuit.

Cardio: Complete 27 minutes of ZT or complete 12 minutes of HIIT.

Cardio Schedule for Week 2

ZT Cardio

Type of training day	MINUTES								
	3	6	9	12	15	18	21	24	27
Resistance training plus cardio	Zone 1	Zone 2	Zone 1	Zone 2	Zone 1	Zone 2	Zone 1		
Cardio only	Zone 1	Zone 2	Zone 1	Zone 2	Zone 1	Zone 2	Zone 1	Zone 2	Zone 1

HIIT Cardio

Type of training day	Total time	Interval instructions
Resistance training plus cardio	8 min.	Alternate between 30 sec. of very intense exercise (such as sprinting) and 20 sec. of lower-intensity activity (such as walking or full rest).
Cardio only	12 min.	Alternate between 30 sec. of very intense exercise (such as sprinting) and 20 sec. of lower-intensity activity (such as walking or full rest).

What's Different This Week?

ZT Cardio is now 20 minutes on resistance-training days and 28 minutes on cardio-only days, and the intervals are now 4 minutes long. In HIIT cardio, the duration of the high-intensity interval increases by 5 seconds. Add one more abdominal exercise on resistance-training days and subtract one on Workout B and the cardio-only days. Do an additional set of the exercises on cardio-only days. Use the table on page 132 to choose ab exercises.

Resistance Training Plus Cardio: Four Days Per Week (Alternating Workouts A and B)

WORKOUT A: DAYS 1 AND 3

Foundational four

Warm-up: Choose two body-weight exercises.

Resistance training: Choose six bilateral exercises.

Ab exercises: Choose six exercises (four for mobility and two for stability). Complete two sets of each; performing all mobility exercises before stability exercises. First, do the four mobility exercises as a circuit with two sets of each. Perform one set of each of the four, one after the other, rest for 60 seconds, and then perform all four of them again for the second set. Next, perform the two stability exercises as supersets, resting for 30 seconds in between.

Cardio: Complete 20 minutes of ZT or complete 8 minutes of HIIT.

WORKOUT B: DAYS 2 AND 4

Foundational four

Warm-up: Choose two body-weight exercises.

Resistance training: Choose six unilateral exercises.

Ab exercises: Choose four exercises (two for mobility and two for stability). Complete two sets of each, performing all mobility exercises before stability exercises. Perform all mobility exercises, then do all the stability exercises. Do both mobility exercises together as supersets, resting for 30 seconds between them. Repeat this pattern for the two stability exercises.

Cardio: Complete 20 minutes of ZT or 8 minutes of HIIT.

Cardio Only: One or Two Days Per Week

Foundational four

Ab exercises: Choose four exercises (two for mobility and two for stability). Choose different exercises than those used for the resistance-training and cardio days. Perform three sets of each, doing the mobility exercises before the stability exercises. Perform both pairs of exercises (the two mobility and the two stability exercises) as supersets, resting 30 seconds or less in between them until you have done all three sets of each exercise.

Cardio: Complete 28 minutes of ZT or 12 minutes of HIIT.

Cardio Schedule for Week 3

ZT Cardio

Type of training day	Minutes						
	4	8	12	16	20	24	28
Resistance training plus cardio	Zone 1	Zone 2	Zone 1	Zone 2	Zone 1		
Cardio only	Zone 1	Zone 2	Zone 1	Zone 2	Zone 1	Zone 2	Zone 1

HIIT Cardio

Type of training day	Total time	Interval instructions
Resistance training plus cardio	8 min.	Alternate between 35 sec. of very intense exercise (such as sprinting) and 20 sec. of lower-intensity activity (such as walking or full rest).
Cardio only	12 min.	Alternate between 35 sec. of very intense exercise (such as sprinting) with 20 sec. of lower-intensity activity (such as walking or full rest).

Sample Workouts

Since week 3 has the most complex schedule for the Rock phase, this section provides examples of workouts A and B. The resistance-training section of workout B include exercises that work one side of the body exclusively. For example, in the single-arm chest press with dumbbells, you hold only one dumbbell. For these types of exercises, you could also hold two dumbbells and alternate your movements to hold one up when the other is down (the dumbbells would pass each other in the middle).

Sample Workout A for Week 3

Workout component	Sample exercises	Additional instruction
Foundational four (see table 8.3)		
Warm-up: Choose 2 body-weight exercises.	Walking lunges: 20 total reps Explosive push-ups: 10 reps	
Resistance training: Choose 6 bilateral exercises.	Superset 1: Upper-body horizontal movements ■ Seated cable row (pull) ■ Dumbbell chest press (push) Superset 2: Lower-body movements ■ Barbell squat (quads) ■ Barbell deadlift (hips) Superset 3: Upper-body vertical movements ■ Pull-up (pull) ■ Dumbbell shoulder press (push)	Do 4 sets of 10 reps, making adjustments to weight as necessary.
Abdominal exercises: Choose 6 exercises (4 for mobility and 2 for stability).	Mobility circuit ■ Reverse crunch on stability ball ■ HTIL crunch ■ Vise crunch with leg roll on stability ball ■ Negative crunch with control Stability superset ■ Leg drop with ball balance ■ Side plank on stability ball	Do 2 sets of each as a circuit; perform all the mobility exercises and then all the stability exercises.
Cardio	ZT: Complete 20 min. (4-min. intervals alternating between zones 1 and 2). HIIT: Complete 8 min. (alternate 35 sec. of high-intensity work with 20 sec. of rest).	

Sample Workout B for Week 3

Workout component	Sample exercises	Additional instruction
Foundational four (see table 8.3)		
Warm-up: Choose 2 body-weight exercises.	Squat-jumps: 20 total reps Mountain climbers: 30 total reps (15 reps per leg)	

Resistance training: Choose 6 unilateral exercises.	Upper-body horizontal movements
	  ■ Standing single-arm row with cable (pull)
	  ■ Single-arm chest press on stability ball with dumbbell (push)
	Lower-body movements
	  ■ Single-leg squat from box or step (quads)
	  ■ Single-straight-leg deadlift with dumbbells (hips)
	Upper-body vertical movements
	  ■ Single-arm pull-down with cable (pull)
	  ■ Standing single-arm shoulder press with dumbbell (push)
		Do 2 sets of 20 reps per side, making adjustments to weight as necessary.

Abdominal exercises: Choose 4 exercises.	Mobility superset
	  ■ TRX V-Up
	  ■ Resisted roll-up with TRX
	Stability superset
	  ■ Leg raise with TRX
	  ■ Plank with elbows on stability ball
		Do 2 sets of each as a superset; perform all the mobility exercises and then all the stability exercises.

Cardio	ZT: Complete 20 min. (4-min. intervals alternating between zones 1 and 2). HIIT: Complete 8 min. (alternate 35 sec. of high-intensity work with 20 sec. of rest).	

Stage 2: Sculpting the Six-Pack

You began chiseling the rock of your abs into a six-pack in chapter 8. This chapter includes the specifics of the Paper phase to continue the sculpting process. You'll continue the cardio plan from chapter 2, incorporate nutrition strategies you identified in chapter 3, and discover complete weekly programs that tie together the ab exercises from chapter 5. In the second part of the Rock, Paper, Scissors theme, you're going to shred the paper! The goal of these workouts is to advance your exercises for strong, well-developed abs and to progress your nutrition modifications and cardio intensity to make the body fat beneath your skin's surface as thin as paper. Simultaneously developing muscle and reducing the fat that's covering it will lead to better abs that are more noticeable.

People who are just getting started with exercise often say they have no abs, but this is impossible. You cannot stand, walk, or do anything else without abs. These people typically mean that their abs are either weak or, more likely, flabby. In many cases, they have perfectly fine abs, especially if they've been working out for years. The muscles are just hidden under a thick layer of body fat. The best training program and ab exercises in the world can give you great abs, but if they are hidden by fat, you're going to be disappointed with how they look. Imagine a field after a large snowfall. It is a uniform blanket of white. To look at it, you would have no idea that underneath the snow, the field is covered in grass. As the weather warms up, the snow cover gets gradually smaller and thinner until a few blades of grass poke through the surface. As the melting continues, more blades of grass become visible. Eventually, only traces of white remain.

Sculpting your abs works in a similar way. You strengthen your abs while eliminating the body fat on top of them until they poke through to the surface.

Of course, unlike snow, the fat in your torso doesn't really melt. Internet ads and infomercials feature products that promise to melt fat, but this is impossible. You don't shed excess body fat the way that a stick of butter melts in a hot pan. These deceptive marketing claims can weaken your resolve. Remember that fat loss is a three-step process of (1) releasing fat from fat cells and (2) delivering it to the muscles to be (3) burned as fuel. Any product, supplement, or program promising anything else is bogus. Change the channel or surf elsewhere. Better yet, go work out or plan some healthy meals for the week.

Placement of Ab Exercises

In the Rock phase in chapter 8, you did the ab exercises (with the exception of the foundational four) at the end of your workouts, as dictated by the rules of physiology. However, this phase of your workouts implements two changes:

1. You will likely no longer need the foundational four as an official, planned part of your program. You can still do them as part of your warm-up, if you like them and feel that they provide a benefit.

2. You will break the rules by doing your ab exercises before your resistance training during workout B.

The foundational four were designed to set the stage for proper abdominal activity by isolating and consciously activating the deeper layers of abdominal muscle. By now, your muscles should be trained to do this automatically when you perform any movement. However, if you enjoy the foundational four and would like to keep doing them, feel free to maintain the same sequence in the workouts. They can help you mentally shift gears as you prepare both your body and mind for the workout.

Next, you'll be breaking the rules with intelligence. Rigid adherence to the rules is for those who aren't smart enough to know when it's okay to break them. In workout B, you use lighter weights and unilateral, asymmetrical loads. Since you don't need to stabilize heavy loads, you can safely prefatigue your abs by doing the targeted ab exercises first. This makes your abs work even harder during resistance training.

Terminology—A Tempest in a Teacup

The terms *abdominals, core,* and *functional training* all fall under the latest trend that is raging in the fitness industry. The debate over the definition of these terms is a tempest in a teacup. Trainers needlessly debate the finer points of these terms while an unfit population gets even more out of shape. For example, chapter 1 discusses the debate over the existence of the upper and lower abs. Does the distinction between six-pack abs and eight-pack abs change the look that you want? Nope. This is one more example of the way people get too caught up in details that don't matter. Whether you can call it a six-pack, an eight-pack, a 40-ounce, or a keg, your goal remains the same. Experts in the fitness industry can have fun with semantic debates over jargon and terminology. Regardless of what you call it, this book helps you get the look you want.

Nutrition

To advance, you need to make better choices on an ongoing basis, and this process also continues with nutrition. It's time to start working on the next couple of items (the third and fourth) from your list of prioritized nutrition changes. These changes will have an important effect on your results. Spending three weeks incorporating them into your new routine will bring you closer to getting the results you want, and will make it easier for you to continue making changes in the next chapter. Why will it get easier? When you are getting results (the feel and the look you want), it is so much easier to do what is necessary and to do it better, more often, and with fewer slipups. When you are living the changes, it's easier to make further improvements because you'll have more desire to improve.

Paper Workout Schedule

The following section outlines your weekly training schedule. As before, each workout starts with a summary of changes for that week so you can move through it quickly and correctly. After the outline of weeks, you'll find sample workouts showing practical applications. Be sure to check out www.AbsRevealed.com for additional information on workouts and exercises.

In the second week of the Rock phase in the chapter 8, you began choosing ab exercises based on whether they provided challenges to stability or mobility. This process continues for all the workouts from now on. The table on page 142 outlines the ab exercises from chapter 5 for the Paper phase.

Since the exercises are getting progressively more challenging and dynamic, you might begin to question the choices of stability or mobility. For example, you will visibly move a lot during the hanging knee raise, but it is listed as a stability challenge. The terms *stability* and *mobility* refer to your abdominal muscles as you perform the exercise. Although your legs move at the hip joint, the abdominals themselves should not move much (only near the top of the movement when your hips roll up slightly). In this exercise, the primary challenge comes from stabilizing your body to prevent swaying or swinging as you move the legs up and down, absorbing the forces that transfer between your moving parts (legs) and your anchor (hands). Although many exercises provide challenges for both stability and mobility, the table lists which of the two characteristics is dominant.

Consider these tips for picking abdominal exercises in the Paper phase:

- Try out new or particularly difficult mobility exercises during workout B. You will be less fatigued at the beginning of the workout, which may lead to more success.

- You can use some, all, or none of the same exercises between workouts A and B. Make your decision based on your preference, available equipment, and ability level.

Ab Exercises From Chapter 5

Exercise name	Primarily stability or mobility	Reps	Exercise page number
BODY-WEIGHT EXERCISES: NO EQUIPMENT			
Reverse crunch (from floor)	Mobility	8-15	70
Reverse crunch (from bench)	Mobility	6-10	71
Frozen bicycle	Mobility	10-20	72
Hanging knee raise (option: add bicycle movement)	Stability	10 (or 10 per leg)	73
Hanging leg raise (option: add scissor movement)	Stability	4-10	74
STABILITY-BALL EXERCISES			
Crunch	Mobility	10-20	75
Offset-arm crunch	Mobility	8-10 per side	76
Crunch with lateral arm swing	Mobility	6-12 per side	77
Crunch with offset torso	Stability	8-12 per side	78
Quad crunch with single leg	Mobility	6-8 per leg (12-16 crunches)	79
Running prone plank	Stability	8-10 per side	80
Lateral rolling plank	Mobility	6-10 per side	81
Plank with knee tuck	Stability	6-10 per side	82
Layout pike	Stability	6-10	83
Hip roll	Mobility	5-8 per side	84
TRX EXERCISES			
Elevated crunch	Stability	10-20	85
Pike	Stability	6-12	86
Elevated mountain climber	Stability	10-15 per leg	87
Elevated crunch and body saw	Stability	6-8	88
Kneeling layout	Stability	8-10	89
Pull-through	Mobility	8-15	90

Resistance Training Plus Cardio: Four Days Per Week (Alternating Workouts A and B)

WORKOUT A: DAYS 1 AND 3

Foundational four (optional)

Warm-up: Choose two body-weight exercises.

Resistance training: Choose six bilateral exercises.

Ab work: Choose six exercises (four for mobility and two for stability). Complete two sets of each.

Cardio: Complete 25 minutes of ZT or 10 minutes of HIIT.

WORKOUT B: DAYS 2 AND 4

Foundational four (optional)

Warm-up: Choose two body-weight exercises.

Ab exercises: Choose four mobility exercises and complete two sets of each.

Resistance training: Choose six unilateral exercises.

Cardio: Complete 25 minutes of ZT or 10 minutes of HIIT.

Cardio Only: One or Two Days Per Week

Ab work: Choose four stability exercises and complete two sets of each as a circuit.

Cardio: Complete 30 minutes of ZT or 14 minutes of HIIT.

Cardio Schedule for Week 1

ZT Cardio

Type of training day	MINUTES					
	5	10	15	20	25	30
Resistance training plus cardio	Zone 1	Zone 2	Zone 1	Zone 2	Zone 1	
Cardio only	Zone 1	Zone 2	Zone 1	Zone 2	Zone 1	Zone 2

HIIT Cardio

Type of training day	Total time	Interval instructions
Resistance training plus cardio	10 min.	Alternate between 30 sec. of very intense exercise (such as sprinting) and 30 sec. of lower-intensity activity (such as walking or full rest).
Cardio only	14 min.	Alternate between 30 sec. of very intense exercise (such as sprinting) and 30 sec. of lower-intensity activity (such as walking or full rest).

What's Different This Week?

ZT cardio is now 24 minutes on resistance-training days. In HIIT cardio, the rest interval decreases by 10 seconds. In workout A, choose five ab exercises for mobility and one for stability. In workout B, choose four ab exercises for mobility. On cardio-only days, choose four ab exercises for stability.

Resistance Training Plus Cardio Days: Four Days Per Week (Alternating Workouts A and B)

WORKOUT A: DAYS 1 AND 3

Foundational four (optional)

Warm-up: Choose two body-weight exercises.

Resistance training: Choose six bilateral exercises.

Ab exercises: Choose six exercises (five for mobility and one for stability). Complete two sets of each.

Cardio: Complete 24 minutes of ZT or 10 minutes of HIIT.

WORKOUT B: DAYS 2 AND 4

Foundational four (optional)

Warm-up: Choose two body-weight exercises.

Ab exercises: Choose four mobility exercises and complete two sets of each.

Resistance training: Choose six unilateral exercises.

Cardio: Complete 24 minutes of ZT or 10 minutes of HIIT.

Cardio Only: One or Two Days Per Week

Ab exercises: Choose four stability exercises and complete two sets of each as a circuit.

Cardio: Complete 30 minutes of ZT or 14 minutes of HIIT.

Cardio Schedule for Week 2

ZT Cardio

Type of training day	MINUTES				
	6	12	18	24	30
Resistance training plus cardio	Zone 1	Zone 2	Zone 1	Zone 2	
Cardio only	Zone 1	Zone 2	Zone 1	Zone 2	Zone 1

HIIT Cardio

Type of training day	Total time	Interval instructions
Resistance training plus cardio	10 min.	Alternate between 30 sec. of very intense exercise (such as sprinting) and 20 sec. of lower-intensity activity (such as walking or full rest).
Cardio only	14 min.	Alternate between 30 sec. of very intense exercise (such as sprinting) and 20 sec. of lower-intensity activity (such as walking or full rest).

What's Different This Week?

ZT cardio is 21 minutes on days of resistance training plus cardio. The interval length for ZT cardio changes for both types of training days. For HIIT cardio, add 1 minute to the total time of cardio-only days. The rest interval moves among 30, 20, and 10 seconds. Until now, you have done cardio-only workouts one or two days per week. This week, go up to two days per week. For ZT cardio, increase intensity by spending more time in zone 2 than in zone 1. However, decrease your total cardio time on resistance-training days to accommodate this change. If you haven't already changed or tried new ab exercises during the first two weeks, do so this week! Dig deep and challenge yourself. Your body is ready for some harder stuff, even if your mind doesn't know it yet.

Resistance Training Plus Cardio: Four Days Per Week (Alternating Workouts A and B)

WORKOUT A: DAYS 1 AND 3

Foundational four (optional)

Warm-up: Complete two body-weight exercises.

Resistance training: Choose six bilateral exercises.

Ab exercises: Choose six exercises (five for mobility and one for stability) and complete two sets of each.

Cardio: Complete 21 minutes of ZT or 10 minutes of HIIT.

WORKOUT B: DAYS 2 AND 4

Foundational four (optional)

Warm-up: Complete two body-weight exercises.

Ab exercises: Choose four mobility exercises and complete two sets of each.

Resistance training: Choose six unilateral exercises.

Cardio: Complete 21 minutes of ZT or 10 minutes of HIIT.

Cardio Only: Two Days Per Week

Ab exercises: Choose four stability exercises and complete two sets of each as a circuit.

Cardio: Complete 30 minutes of ZT or 15 minutes of HIIT.

Cardio Schedule for Week 3

ZT Cardio

Type of training day	MINUTES						
	3	9	12	18	21	27	30
Resistance training plus cardio	Zone 1	Zone 2	Zone 1	Zone 2	Zone 1		
Cardio only	Zone 1	Zone 2	Zone 1	Zone 2	Zone 1	Zone 2	Zone 1

HIIT Cardio

Type of training day	Total time	Interval instructions
Resistance training plus cardio	10 min.	Alternate between 30 sec. of very intense exercise (such as sprinting) with an interval of lower-intensity activity (such as walking or full rest). Choose from 30, 20, and 10 sec. for the rest interval.
Cardio only	15 min.	Alternate between 30 sec. of very intense exercise (such as sprinting) and an interval of lower-intensity activity (such as walking or full rest). Choose from 30, 20, and 10 sec. for the rest interval.

Sample Workouts

The sample workouts that follow provide examples of workouts A and B for week 2. The resistance-training exercises have been changed to give you more options. You will also find sample ab exercises for the cardio-only day of week 2.

Sample Workout A for Week 2

Workout component	Sample exercises	Additional instruction
Foundational four (see page 129)		Optional
Warm-up: Choose 2 exercises.	Walking lunges: 20 total reps Explosive push-ups: 10 reps	
Resistance training: Choose 6 bilateral exercises.	Superset 1: Upper-body horizontal movements • Barbell row (pull) • Barbell chest press (push) Superset 2: Lower-body movements • Leg press (quads) • Barbell straight-leg deadlift (hips) Superset 3: Upper-body vertical movements • Chin-up (pull) • Standing shoulder press with barbell (push)	Do 4 sets of 10 reps, making adjustments to weight as necessary.
Abdominal exercises: Choose 6 exercises (5 for mobility and 1 for stability).	Mobility circuit • Frozen bicycle • Offset-arm crunch on stability ball • Lateral rolling plank on stability ball • Hip roll on stability ball • Quad crunch with single leg Stability exercise • Running prone plank on stability ball	Complete 2 sets of each as a circuit.
Cardio	ZT: Complete 24 min. (6-min. intervals alternating between zones 1 and 2). HIIT: Complete 10 min. (alternate 30 sec. of high-intensity exercise with 20 sec. of rest).	

Sample Workout B for Week 2

Workout component	Sample exercises	Additional instruction
Foundational four (see page 129)		Optional
Warm-up: Choose 2 body-weight exercises.	Squat jump: 20 total reps Mountain climber: 30 total reps (15 reps per leg)	
Resistance training: Choose 6 unilateral exercises.	Upper-body horizontal movements ■ Standing single-arm row with dumbbell (pull) ■ Standing single-arm chest press with cable (push) Lower-body movements ■ Single-leg squat: From box or step (quads) ■ Suitcase deadlift with barbell: Hold the middle of the barbell with one hand (hips) Upper-body vertical movements ■ Single arm pull-down with cable (pull) ■ Standing single-arm shoulder press with dumbbell (push)	Do 2 sets of 20 reps per side, making adjustments to weight as necessary.
Abdominal exercises: Choose 4 mobility exercises.	Mobility exercises ■ Offset-arm crunch on stability ball ■ Reverse crunch from bench ■ Hip roll on stability ball ■ Crunch on stability ball	Do 2 sets of each as superset pairs or do a circuit with all 4 of your choice of mobility exercises.
Cardio	ZT: Complete 24 min. (6-min. intervals alternating between zones 1 and 2). HIIT: Complete 10 min. (alternate 30 sec. of high-intensity exercise with 20 sec. of rest).	

Sample Ab Exercises for Cardio-Only Days

Workout component	Sample exercises	Additional instruction
Abdominal exercises: Choose 4 stability exercises.	Stability exercises ■ Layout pike on stability ball ■ Elevated crunch and body saw with TRX ■ Elevated mountain climber with TRX ■ Kneeling layout with TRX	Do 2 sets of each as a circuit.

That's it for the Paper phase. Don't forget to smash the clock with the emergency plan introduced in chapter 8 if time is running short and you need to get your workout in.

CHAPTER 10

Stage 3: Polishing to Perfection

It's time to get cut with the Scissors phase, the final part of our Rock, Paper, Scissors theme. By now, you have six solid weeks of training and making nutritional changes under your belt. You should also have less body fat and better abs for noticeable results. The goal of these workouts is to advance your abdominal exercises and to progress your nutritional modifications and cardio intensity, strengthening and developing your abs while cutting the body fat beneath the surface of your skin. Your strong, stable abs will get even better as they become more visible. In the final four weeks, you'll dial in the results that will give you abs you can be truly proud of.

You've done some very challenging ab work in the Rock and Paper phases. The Scissors phase incorporates the exercises from chapter 6. Many of these challenging, cutting-edge exercises were created exclusively for this program. Every single one provides big challenges, combining spinal flexion, extension, and rotation for either mobility or stability.

Placement of Ab Exercises

In the first two weeks of the Scissors phase, you will ignore the rules of ab training completely. This means that for both workouts A and B, you will perform the abdominal exercises before your resistance-training exercises. To accommodate this change in order, do not increase the resistance on any of your resistance-training exercises during week 1. Performing the ab exercises first will make everything that follows a little harder than you are used to. By week 2, apply the principle of training for the feeling rather than for the number (see chapter 8 for more information) during your resistance-training workouts. Feel free to increase the resistance if needed during this week.

As before, the foundational four are no longer an official part of your program. However, you can still do them as part of your warm-up if you find them beneficial.

Nutrition

By now, you've made the main changes to your nutritional habits from your prioritized list, and you should already see and feel the results. Still, a little taste of progress can drive you to achieve more, since it unlocks the potential for your abs. Keep going by picking two more items from your list of prioritized nutritional changes. Specifically, work on the remaining items on your list. Although this should be getting easier (the first items represented bigger changes to your daily habits), you may still encounter challenges. Changing your nutritional habits for the better in a world that values cheap, worthless food designed to taste good rather than provide nourishment will be a lifelong battle.

It's time to man up, and you can do it because anyone can do it. Everyone possesses the ability to make better choices. Some people make them and some do not —the evidence is visible in the bodies you see as you go about your day. This is not a criticism. Unhealthy, unfit bodies that neither look appealing nor perform well are the inevitable result of poor choices. In the same way, healthy and fit bodies that perform at a high level are the inevitable result of wise choices.

The time is now. Start working on the remaining items on your prioritized nutritional list.

Scissors Workout Schedule

This section outlines your weekly training schedules. As before, each workout begins with a summary of changes for that week so you can move through it quickly and correctly. After the weekly outlines, you'll find a sample workout illustrating practical applications.

When choosing ab exercises for your Scissors workouts, you can use some, all, or none of the same exercises for workouts A and B. Decide based on your preferences, available equipment, and ability level. The table on page 151 outlines ab exercises from chapter 6 for the Scissors phase.

For resistance-training days during the Scissors phase, you may add an exercise to workouts A and B for one or two muscles or areas of your body that need further strengthening. By now, you should be familiar enough with the format of the workouts to move through them quickly. Use your extra time to add exercises for particular areas you'd like to focus on. You may also choose to stick with the original program if you feel your muscular development is well balanced. However, if you'd like to strengthen or develop one or two areas of your body, you now have an option that fits your workout plan. These additions should be based on what you see as areas of muscular deficiency. For example, if you wanted to strengthen your back, and you were already doing pull-ups in workout A and single-arm pull-downs with cable in workout B, you could add one back exercise to each workout. For example, you could add chin-ups to workout A and a

Ab Exercises From Chapter 6

Exercise name	Primarily stability or mobility	Reps	Exercise page number
EXERCISES USING BODY WEIGHT AND BASIC EQUIPMENT			
Bicycle crunch	Mobility	8-12 per side	93
Flying bicycle crunch with medicine ball	Stability	8-12 per side	94
Hanging knee raise with a twist	Mobility	4-6 per side	95
Bar chop (with light barbell or weighted bar)	Mobility	10-15 per side	96
Standing oblique crunch with cable	Mobility	10-15 per side	97
STABILITY-BALL EXERCISES			
Kickboxer crunch	Stability	8-12 per side	98
Plank with cross-body knee tuck	Stability	6-10 per side	99
Rotating crunch with lateral arm swing	Mobility	6-10 per side	100
Hip roll with thread the needle	Mobility	5-10 per side	101
TRX EXERCISES			
Elevated oblique crunch	Mobility	8-12 per side	102
Pendulum pike	Stability	6-12 per side	103
Pendulum mountain climber	Mobility	10-20 per leg	104
Hip roll with thread the needle	Mobility	5-10 per side	105
Side plank with reach-through	Mobility	5-10 per side	106
Side plank with tuck	Stability	8-12 per side	107
Oblique V-up	Stability	5-10 per side	108
EXERCISES WITH SLIDE AND BOSU			
BOSU double crunch	Stability	8-15	109
Twisting-knee tuck with slide	Mobility	6-10 per side	110
Side-plank tuck with slide	Mobility	8-15 per side	111
Twisting-hip pike with slide	Mobility	8-15 per side	112
Mountain climber with slide	Stability	10-20 per leg	113

single straight-arm push-down with a cable to workout B. In the workout plans that follow, this option is reflected as *six to eight exercises* during the resistance-training portion of the workout.

The next challenge for your cardiorespiratory training will be staying in zone 2 for a steady-state (consistent-intensity) effort. This contrasts with the intervals used at the beginning of the program. Recall that in the Rock phase, you spent equal amounts of time in zones 1 and 2. Toward the end of the Paper phase, the length of the intervals changed so that you spent a longer amount of time in zone 2 than in zone 1. This progression continues at the beginning of the Scissors phase. By the end of it, you'll be performing entire cardiorespiratory training sessions in zone 2. You'll even briefly perform intervals at intensities above zone 2. Visit www.AbsRevealed.com for additional information on workouts and exercises.

WEEK 1 (WEEK 7 OVERALL)

What's Different This Week?

Your abdominal exercises are placed before resistance-training exercises for workouts A and B. As a result, maintain the resistance set out in week 3 of the Paper phase for all resistance-training exercises.

Resistance Training Plus Cardio: Four Days Per Week (Alternating Workouts A and B)

WORKOUT A: DAYS 1 AND 3

Foundational four (optional)

Warm-up: Choose two body-weight exercises.

Ab exercises: Choose six exercises (four for mobility and two for stability) and complete two sets of each.

Resistance training: Choose six to eight bilateral exercises.

Cardio: Complete 20 to 25 minutes of ZT or 10 minutes of HIIT.

WORKOUT B: DAYS 2 AND 4

Foundational four (optional)

Warm-up: Choose two body-weight exercises.

Ab exercises: Choose four exercises (two for mobility and two for stability) and complete two sets of each.

Resistance training: Choose six to eight unilateral exercises.

Cardio: Complete 20 to 25 minutes of ZT or 10 minutes of HIIT.

Cardio Only: One or Two Days Per Week

Cardio Schedule for Week 1

ZT Cardio

	MINUTES			
Type of training day	2	8	10	To end (10-15 min. from end of prior interval from zone 1)
Resistance training plus cardio	Zone 1	Zone 2	Zone 1	Zone 2
Cardio only	Zone 1	Zone 2	Zone 1	Zone 2

HIIT Cardio

Type of training day	Total time	Interval instructions
Resistance training plus cardio	10 min.	Alternate between 30 sec. of very intense exercise (such as sprinting) and 20 sec. of lower-intensity activity (such as walking or full rest).
Cardio only	15 min.	Alternate between 30 sec. of very intense exercise (such as sprinting) and 20 sec. of lower-intensity activity (such as walking or full rest).

What's Different This Week?

ZT cardio is now 20 minutes on days of resistance training and cardio only. Spend the entire workout in zone 2. HIIT cardio does not change. You can resume adding resistance as necessary to any resistance-training exercise.

Resistance Training Plus Cardio: Four Days Per Week (Alternating Workouts A and B)

WORKOUT A: DAYS 1 AND 3

Foundational four (optional)

Warm-up: Choose two body-weight exercises.

Ab exercises: Choose six exercises (four for mobility and two for stability) and complete two sets of each.

Resistance training: Choose six to eight bilateral exercises.

Cardio: Complete 20 minutes of ZT (zone 2 only) or 10 minutes of HIIT.

WORKOUT B: DAYS 2 AND 4

Foundational four (optional)

Warm-up: Choose two body-weight exercises.

Ab exercises: Choose four exercises (two for mobility and two for stability) and complete two sets of each.

Resistance training: Choose six to eight unilateral exercises.

Cardio: Complete 20 minutes of ZT (zone 2 only) or 10 minutes of HIIT.

Cardio Only: One or Two Days Per Week

Ab exercises: Choose four exercises and do two sets of each as a circuit.

Cardio: Complete 20 minutes of ZT (zone 2 only) or 15 minutes of HIIT.

Cardio Schedule for Week 2

ZT Cardio

	MINUTES
Type of training day	20
Resistance training plus cardio	Zone 2
Cardio only	Zone 2

HIIT Cardio

Type of training day	Total time	Interval instructions
Resistance training plus cardio	10 min.	Alternate between 30 sec. of very intense exercise (such as sprinting) and 20 sec. of lower-intensity activity (such as walking or full rest).
Cardio only	15 min.	Alternate between 30 sec. of very intense exercise (such as sprinting) and 20 sec. of lower-intensity activity (such as walking or full rest).

WEEK 3 (WEEK 9 OVERALL)

What's Different This Week?

ZT cardio changes to 25 to 30 minutes on cardio-only days. On these days, follow this structure: Do four minutes in zone 2, one minute above zone 2, one minute in zone 1, and four minutes in zone 2. Repeat this pattern until the end of your workout time. For HIIT cardio, the duration of the high-intensity interval increases by 10 seconds. In workout B, only perform ab exercises for mobility, and choose new exercises. In workout A, place the abdominal exercises after resistance training.

Resistance Training Plus Cardio: Four Days Per Week (Alternating Workouts A and B)

WORKOUT A: DAYS 1 AND 3

Foundational four (optional)

Warm-up: Choose two body-weight exercises.

Resistance training: Choose six to eight bilateral exercises.

Ab exercises: Choose six exercises (four for mobility and two for stability) and complete two sets of each.

Cardio: Complete 20 minutes of ZT (zone 2 only) or 10 minutes of HIIT.

WORKOUT B: DAYS 2 AND 4

Foundational four (optional)

Warm-up: Choose two body-weight exercises.

Ab exercises: Choose four mobility exercises and complete two sets of each.

Resistance training: Choose six to eight unilateral exercises.

Cardio: Complete 20 minutes of ZT (zone 2 only) or 10 minutes of HIIT.

Cardio Only: One or Two Days Per Week

Ab exercises: Choose four stability exercises and complete two sets of each as a circuit.

Cardio: Complete 25 to 30 minutes of ZT or 15 minutes of HIIT.

Cardio Schedule for Week 3

ZT Cardio

Type of training day	MINUTES						
	20						
Resistance training plus cardio	Zone 2						
	4	5	6	10	11	12	16*
Cardio only	Zone 2	> zone 2	Zone 1	Zone 2	> zone 2	Zone 1	Zone 2

*Repeat pattern to end of workout time (25-30 min. total).

HIIT Cardio

Type of training day	Total time	Interval instructions
Resistance training plus cardio	10 min.	Alternate between 40 sec. of very intense exercise (such as sprinting) and 20 sec. of lower-intensity activity (such as walking or full rest).
Cardio only	15 min.	Alternate between 40 sec. of very intense exercise (such as sprinting) and 20 sec. of lower-intensity activity (such as walking or full rest).

WEEK 4 (WEEK 10 OVERALL)

What's Different This Week?

For ZT cardio on cardio-only days, follow this structure: Do five minutes in zone 2, one minute above zone 2, and five minutes in zone 2. Repeat this pattern until the end of your workout. For HIIT cardio, your rest interval changes among 30, 20, and 10 seconds.

Resistance Training Plus Cardio: Four Days Per Week (Alternating Workouts A and B)

WORKOUT A: DAYS 1 AND 3

Foundational four (optional)

Warm-up: Choose two body-weight exercises.

Resistance training: Choose six to eight bilateral exercises.

Ab exercises: Choose six exercises (four for mobility and two for stability) and complete two sets of each.

Cardio: Complete 20 minutes of ZT (zone 2 only) or 10 minutes of HIIT.

WORKOUT B: DAYS 2 AND 4

Foundational four (optional)

Warm-up: Choose two body-weight exercises.

Ab exercises: Choose four mobility exercises and complete two sets of each.

Resistance training: Choose six to eight unilateral exercises.

Cardio: Complete 20 minutes of ZT (zone 2 only) or 10 minutes of HIIT.

Cardio Only: One or Two Days Per Week

Ab exercises: Choose four stability exercises and complete two sets of each as a circuit.

Cardio: Complete 25 to 30 minutes of ZT or 15 minutes of HIIT.

Cardio Schedule for Week 4

ZT Cardio

Type of training day	MINUTES				
	20				
Resistance training plus cardio	Zone 2				
	5	6	11	12	17*
Cardio only	Zone 2	> zone 2	Zone 2	> zone 2	Zone 2

*Repeat pattern to end of workout time (25-30 min. total).

HIIT Cardio

Type of training day	Total time	Interval instructions
Resistance training plus cardio	15 min.	Alternate between 40 sec. of very intense exercise (such as sprinting) with an interval of lower-intensity activity (such as walking or full rest) that rotates among 30, 20, and 10 sec.
Cardio only	15 min.	Alternate between 40 sec. of very intense exercise (such as sprinting) and an interval of lower-intensity activity (such as walking or full rest) that rotates among 30, 20, and 10 sec.

Sample Workouts

Below you will find sample workouts for week 1 with the exercises filled in. You have workouts A and B, plus sample ab exercises for the cardio-only day. Feel free to experiment a bit with other resistance-training exercises. By now, you're quite strong and quite capable, so please don't limit yourself to the sample exercises during resistance training.

Sample Workout A for Week 1

Workout component	Sample exercise	Additional instruction
Foundational four		Optional
Warm-up: Choose 2 body-weight exercises.	Walking lunges: 20 total reps Explosive push-ups: 10 reps	
Abdominal exercises: Choose 6 exercises (4 for mobility and 2 for stability).	Mobility circuit ■ Rotating crunch with lateral arm swing on stability ball ■ Hip roll with thread-the-needle on stability ball ■ Hanging knee raise with a twist ■ Bar chop (with light barbell) Stability exercises ■ Flying bicycle crunch (with medicine ball) ■ Plank with knee tuck (opposite elbow)	Do 2 sets of each as a circuit.
Resistance training: Choose 6-8 bilateral exercises.	Superset 1: Upper-body horizontal movements ■ Barbell row (pull) ■ Barbell chest press (push) Superset 2: Lower-body movements ■ Barbell squat (quads) ■ Barbell deadlift (hips) Superset 3: Upper-body vertical movements ■ Pull-up (pull) ■ Standing shoulder press with barbell (push)	Do 4 sets of 10 reps from the final week of Paper workouts without changing weight.
Cardio	ZT: Complete 20-25 min. For the first 10 min. move between zones 1 & 2 as instructed. Complete the final 10-15 min. in zone 2. HIIT: Complete 10 min. Alternate 30 sec. of high-intensity work with 20 sec. of rest.	

Sample Workout B for Week 1

Workout component	Sample exercise	Additional instruction
Foundational four		Optional
Warm-up: Choose 2 body-weight exercises.	Squat jump: 20 total reps Mountain climber: 30 total reps (15 reps per leg)	
Abdominal exercises: Choose 4 exercises (2 for mobility and 2 for stability).	Mobility exercises ■ TRX side plank with reach-through ■ Elevated oblique crunch with TRX Stability exercises ■ Pendulum pike with TRX ■ Oblique V-up with TRX	Choose between performing 2 sets of mobility and stability exercises grouped as superset pairs or a circuit of all 4 exercises.
Resistance training: Choose 6-8 unilateral exercises.	Upper-body horizontal movements ■ Standing single-arm row with dumbbell (pull) ■ Standing single-arm chest press with cable (push) Lower-body movements ■ Single-leg squat: Perform from box or step (quads) ■ Suitcase deadlift with barbell: Hold the middle of the barbell with one hand (hips) Upper-body vertical movements ■ Single-arm pull-down with cable (pull) ■ Standing single-arm shoulder press with dumbbell (push)	Do 2 sets of 20 reps per side without making adjustments to weight.
Cardio	ZT: Complete 20-25 min. For the first 10 min., vary between zones 1 & 2 as instructed. Perform the final 10-15 min. in zone 2. HIIT: Complete 10 min. Alternate 30 sec. of high-intensity work with 20 sec. of rest.	

Sample Abdominal Exercises for Cardio-Only Workouts

Workout component	Sample exercise	Additional instruction
Abdominal exercises: Choose 4 exercises.	Stability exercises ■ Twisting-knee tuck with slide ■ Twisting-hip pike with slide ■ Mountain climber on stability ball ■ Kickboxer crunch on stability ball	Do 2 sets of each as a circuit.

That's it for the Scissors phase. As always, smash the clock with the emergency workout plan if time is running short and you need to get your workout in.

Get great abs in 10 weeks by chiseling the rock, shredding the paper, and getting cut with the scissors. Unlike a game of rock, paper, scissors, there's nothing random about the plan laid out for you. You know what you need to do and you know how to modify your nutritional habits to reveal the great abs you built during the 10 weeks of training.

Next, you will discover strategies for maintaining the great progress you have made. Once you get great abs, why give them up? Now that you know how to continually challenge your body, permanently improve your nutritional habits, and handle those days when life interrupts your workout plans, there is no reason that you can't sustain results.

CHAPTER 11

Stage 4: Maintaining Your Results

This book's approach to fitness is to get it and then keep it. Fitness is not complicated. It might not be easy to attain, but it isn't complicated. Here's a popular maxim from personal finance: It's not how much you make, but how much you keep that matters. The same could be said for fitness. It's not really how fit you get, but how fit you remain that matters. Achieving a high level of fitness takes more work to get there initially than it does to keep it. Maintaining is easier than changing. This chapter gives you the strategies for keeping the great abs you've worked so hard to get. Successfully maintaining what you've gained takes both mental and physical strength.

Mental Maintenance

One of the most dangerous times in any fitness plan is when you have almost reached your goal. When you are nearly there, you begin reaping many of the rewards of achieving the goal, such as a stronger body with more visible muscles and abs, and all the confidence that results. At this time, it's easy to let your guard down, relax, and slowly slide back into old habits that will take you away from your goal. You might be out with friends at happy hour and reward yourself by eating or drinking foods that aren't in your nutrition plan. All of a sudden, you relax a little more here and a little more there, and you wind up going backward or maybe sliding back into old bad habits completely. Once that happens, it's hard to get back on track.

Life is full of ups and downs with jobs and relationships. You can't expect everything to go perfectly in life all the time. Fitness is no different, but many people act as if it is. When you have a bad day in fitness, pick up where you left off and move on. Just let it go. Once a workout is missed, it's gone forever, so all you can do is move forward. Just as a few good workouts don't completely transform your body, a few missed workouts won't make you out of shape. The disaster is letting a few bad days become a few bad months. Make the most of the times where everything clicks and use them to get as fit as you can. When setbacks occur, and they will occur, treat them as you would in every other area of life! It really is that simple. Don't overanalyze it and don't beat yourself up over it. Just keep going forward.

You can exercise, get fit, and get great abs, all while maintaining an outside life. Many people erroneously believe that fitness requires an austere level of commitment and dedication that sucks all the fun out of life. You have to do what is needed for results, but the necessary commitment isn't as extensive as many people think. You don't need to work out several hours each day and you don't need to live on sprouts and protein shakes alone. Life is meant to be lived, and the best way to do that is in a fit body. However, the pursuit of fitness does not need to take over your life. Even at high levels of fitness, unless you're competing for an endurance event, if your workouts are taking longer than 90 minutes, you're probably not working hard enough.

If you find yourself becoming dissatisfied with your results, ask yourself some questions. Are you doing anything to limit your progress? Are you failing to do something that's holding you back? Answer these questions honestly instead of just deciding to do more. Many people make the error of doing more of the same workout that isn't getting them what they want. Often, the intensity is lacking in either resistance training or cardio. They are simply going through the motions. Adding 10 more minutes of ineffective training is not the solution. When in doubt, use the methods in the following section to add intensity to your workouts rather than time, and you will find that your progress resumes.

Physical Maintenance

The resistance-training exercises in your workouts focus on your torso, hips, and thighs. You get the most bang for your buck this way, both in terms of the physical response in your body and in terms of the best use of your time. Consider the following summary of this concept: Always choose exercises that use muscles from the hips to the armpits. If you choose exercises that involve the muscles in your torso, hips, and thighs, you'll be using the most calories during the workout. You'll also get the biggest metabolic response from your body by activating more muscle tissue.

Over time, you'll want to try new exercises or variations of current ones. As long as you follow the preceding rule, you'll continue to get results from your workout. Suppose you give each of two identical twins four exercises to do. One twin gets squats, deadlifts, push-ups, and pull-ups. The other twin gets biceps curls, triceps extensions, calf raises, and lateral raises. Which one do you think will have the best overall physical response to the training? The answer is the first twin, of course. No one has ever reshaped their bodies by performing only biceps curls, calf raises, and other exercises that involve relatively small amounts of muscle. If you have the time and the inclination, you can always add these types of exercises to your workouts, but they should never be the foundation of your training.

Erase the Finish Line

Yes, it takes ongoing and consistent effort to maintain fitness, but that's just because your body is smart. In its quest for efficiency, it will not keep muscles around that it isn't using. Remember, your body is governed by the simple rule of stimulus and response. This has big implications for your fitness program. If you give your body a reason to keep muscle around, it will do so. If you take away the reason, the body will get rid of the muscle because it costs too much (in terms of energy) to maintain. However, humans have their limits. Consistent exercise done in a linear fashion does not result in infinite strength. If this were true, years of performing shoulder presses would enable us to lift cars over our heads. A realistic strategy for challenging your muscles is critical to maintaining your progress. You can use any of the following techniques to confuse your body and maintain your results:

- Change your exercises for resistance training and abdominal training.
- Change the order of your exercises for resistance training and abdominal training.
- Increase the number of reps performed with the same weight.
- Reduce the amount of rest between sets.
- Try a variation of an exercise you are already performing.

It should be fairly straightforward to use different exercises. Switching up the order is a terrific and easy way to make your workouts feel different. In this text, you use 10 reps in workout A and 20 reps in workout B. You could use six reps in A and 15 in B, or any other combination, to create variety. There's nothing magical about the exact reps outlined in the book. Taking less time between sets is another terrific way to add intensity and to save time. (It also helps you cut down on needless chitchat during workouts.) Varying the way you do an exercise is another simple change that helps you maintain progress. For example, if you currently perform an overhead press with dumbbells while seated on a bench, try performing them with the same weight while standing. This will definitely make you work harder! In fact, the first time you stand up, you may even have to decrease the weight. This is because the change in the overall demand to your body, specifically to your abs for stability, can make the same weight feel significantly more challenging. In short, anything that gives your muscles a novel challenge supplies the stimulus for change.

Cardio Quality

As you get to the end of your 10-week program, you'll want to repeat your test for VT1 HR. As a result of your training, your VT1 HR will have changed. Your heart should now be able to work at higher intensities with less effort. Consider this analogy of a car: A beat-up clunker may struggle to get up to 70 mph (113 kmph), but a sports car can handle 70 mph easily. Since your body has moved from the condition of a clunker to that of a sports car, your heart's point of VT1 crossover will have moved higher as well. Look at it another way: Imagine you had a car with an engine that could learn to be more fuel efficient over time simply by being driven. If this happened, the car would use progressively less and less fuel for the same distance. With regular training, your body also becomes more efficient. The same effort (for speed, resistance, and time) requires fewer calories from your body.

The result for your body is that your crossover point (where your body switches from burning a majority of fat for fuel to burning a majority of carbohydrate) moves up. This means that you can exercise with greater effort and burn a higher number of calories while accessing more fat for fuel. Of course, in order to actually train above the crossover point now (zone 2), you'll be working even harder than you have before. This process does not continue forever, however. You will reach a point where you maintain results with your cardio workouts as well. When you are happy with your results (you have the look you want and a body that is ready for action), you don't need to push the boundaries anymore.

Nutrition for a Lifetime

As you checked items off your list of prioritized nutrition changes, you felt better, reduced body fat, and added muscle. This process will continue for as long as you continue to improve. To be your best, you will always be in pursuit of ways to do things a little better, such as consuming unhealthy foods a little less frequently and eating healthy foods a little more frequently. As new scientific research emerges, you will change and adapt along with it. Just don't expect any shocking changes. Although many people are confused by nutrition, we all know that we should eat more fruits, veggies, lean proteins, beans, nuts, and healthy fat and that we should avoid junk food, sweets, and unhealthy fat.

This premise of healthy foods hasn't changed much. Fads, extreme diets, government regulations that are often decades behind the research, and clever advertising disguised as information are responsible for the confusion. The flow of information and misinformation comes at us from all sides all the time. Anytime you're feeling confused and frustrated by something you read or heard about nutrition, just go back to the basics of healthy eating.

Once again, the proper mindset is a critical part of successfully navigating the world of nutrition. Those who get confused by nutrition are often the same people who treat themselves with unhealthy foods to mark one event or another, who always hit the office candy dish, and who must have something sweet after a meal. Please don't be one of them. The enjoyment and satisfaction of living in a body that is capable, not to mention appealing to look at, are a powerful way to keep you connected to the value of consistently good choices. By now, you are living proof that making smart nutrition choices leaves you looking better than you thought possible and feeling better than you should be allowed to feel without narcotics!

Never forget this: The best workout in the world cannot deliver the great abs you want if you do not support it with excellent nutrition. You might work out every day, but you eat several times a day. You have many opportunities to give your body better materials for the daily construction project of every cell in your body.

Lots of people out there who want great abs use a random approach. They might do lots of ab exercises or lots of cardio, follow an extreme diet, or buy some piece of equipment from an infomercial in the middle of the night that promises results in only minutes a day. These attempts to get great abs never deliver results because they lack strategy. Nothing in this book is random. You start with the rock of your body and chisel it down. You shred body fat down to paper-thin layers, and you get cut with scissors. No efforts are wasted. By systematically using a strategy to train your body and to feed it properly, you are guaranteed to get great abdominals.

Ten Key Concepts

The following concepts are the big ideas to lock in and keep close at hand so you get the best-looking abs and a body that is healthy and ready for action. Consider this your top 10 list of *Abs Revealed* concepts:

1. Training your abdominals with movement is just as important as training them by preventing movement.
2. Your inner and outer abs work together to create and allow all of your movements.
3. Eating healthy fat in the right amounts puts less fat on your body.
4. Eating sugar and refined, processed carbohydrate and grains puts more fat on your body.
5. Your eating habits will never be perfect, but you should never stop working to make them better.
6. Great abdominals do not just come from abdominal exercises; they also come from a sound, full-body workout plan.
7. The recipe for great abdominals is to train hard and smart, have fun, eat right, and recover. Let nothing distract you from this.
8. Sometimes breaking the rules of abdominal training makes sense.
9. Successful workouts make you feel comfortably uncomfortable.
10. When doing resistance training, train for the feeling of fatigue in the muscle rather than for the number of reps.

Check out the book's Web site for additional information and updates. May you achieve the results you deserve from your efforts! Hard work with the wrong tools leads to a lot of frustration, but your hard work will yield the reward of the abs you've wanted. Every accomplishment is a new starting point for making yourself better.

Jonathan Ross is an award-winning figure in the world of fitness. He is the owner of Aion Fitness, which provides fitness training, writing, speaking, and consulting services. He also is the personal training director at Sport Fit Total Fitness in Bowie, Maryland.

Ross has been featured in *Shape, Fitness, Tennis, Women's Health, Cooking Light*, WebMD, and the *Washington Post*. He is a two-time Personal Trainer of the Year (2010 IDEA Health & Fitness Association and 2006 American Council on Exercise) for his creativity and strong leadership in the fitness industry. His career is inspired by his family history of obesity and his "800 pounds of parents," as he often characterizes them. He is a fitness expert for Discovery Health, where he hosts the video series *Everyday Fitness with Jonathan Ross*. He was voted the 2008 Best Personal Trainer by Exercise TV and listed as one of the Top 100 Trainers in America by *Men's Journal* magazine.

A former astronomer, Ross used to study stellar bodies; now he builds them! His favorite activities are hiking, tennis, football, and volleyball—almost any sport involving chasing a ball or a person. He relaxes with music and enjoys caring for saltwater and freshwater fish. Ross lives just outside Washington, DC.